GLOBAL WITNESSES TO PENTECOST

THE TESTIMONY OF 'OTHER TONGUES'

GLOBAL WITNESSES TO PENTECOST

THE TESTIMONY OF 'OTHER TONGUES'

JORDAN DANIEL MAY

Cherohala Press
Cleveland, Tennessee

Global Witnesses to Pentecost
The Testimony of 'Other Tongues'

Published by Cherohala Press
An imprint of CPT Press
900 Walker ST NE
Cleveland, TN 37311
email: cptpress@pentecostaltheology.org
website: www.pentecostaltheology.org

Library of Congress Control Number 2012954662
ISBN-10 1935931326
ISBN-13 9781935931324

Cover: 'Pentecost' by Titian (Tiziano Vecelli), c. 1545

To Reverend B.H. Clendennen
(05/22/1922 – 12/13/2009),
founding pastor,
Victory Temple Assembly of God, Beaumont, TX,
founding president,
School of Christ International,
a true apostle of Pentecost
and missionary to the world

TABLE OF CONTENTS

ACKNOWLEDGEMENTS

Throughout the writing of this book I received encouraging words, inspiration, and support from many friends and colleagues. Charles Lyons, former Pastor of Bethel Assembly of God, Jacksonville, NC, was a great inspiration during the beginning stages and an encouragement throughout. Dr Doyle Jones, Worldwide Evangelist, and Christopher Houston, Correctional Chaplain and Pastor of Bridge of Life Community Fellowship, encouraged me during some of the project's low points.

Other friends and colleagues who offered their support and advice include: Dr L. John Bueno (retired Executive Director, Assemblies of God World Missions), Dr Charles Kelly (Superintendent, North Carolina District of the Assemblies of God), Dr Adonna Otwell (Professor and Department Chair, General Studies, Southwestern Assemblies of God University), Mark Scafidi (Pastor, First Assembly of God, Pennington, NJ), Jeff Holt (Pastor, Levesque Assembly of God, Wynne, AR), Jeremy Crenshaw (PhD student, Regent University), Rick Giannico (Worship Pastor, Glad Tidings Church, St. Petersburg, FL), Tim Kalapis (member, First Assembly of God, Pennington, NJ), Craig S. Keener (Professor, Asbury Theological Seminary), Leon D. Parker (Correctional Chaplain), Dan Son (Correctional Chaplain), Dr Charles Gaulden (Associate Professor of Religion, Southeastern University), Don Brankel (Evangelist, Arkansas District of the Assemblies of God), and Ed and Betty Marcontell (Capstone Ministries, Rusk, TX).

I also wish to thank three biblical scholars who have greatly shaped my theology regarding Luke-Acts: Roger Stronstad, Jim Shelton, and Bob Menzies. The fingerprints of your scholarship are ever present throughout my studies.

Of course, I have to thank all those who prayed for the project and those who contributed testimonies to it. Your prayers are appreciated and your witness is a great testimony to the Lord's power and Spirit's presence. Thank you for the opportunity to publish your stories. In the words of the Apostle Paul, 'For the Spirit God gave us does not make us timid ... *So do not be ashamed of the testimony about our Lord* ...' (2 Tim. 1.7-8 NIV, emphasis added).

Jordan Daniel May
Pentecost 2012
Raleigh, NC

FOREWORD

A pastor once told me that when he was a child in 1955, his dad was the Sunday School Superintendent in Luxor, AR. His father took him to the small church, along with a guest who was to speak that evening – a missionary who had returned from China six years earlier. It was a custom for there to be prayer before the service, with the men going into one room and the women another. As they entered, an old grandma in the women's prayer room was praying in the Spirit. The missionary listened awhile and then said, 'That lady is praying for the members of my church in China, and calling out every name'. The missionary was my dad.

While we do not build our theology on experience, supernatural experiences like these certainly validate our theology as the Day of Pentecost fulfilled and validated 'what was spoken by the prophet Joel' (Acts 2.16). The late Dr Gary McGee used the term 'experience certified theology' to describe such signs and wonders.

Jesus promised his disciples that they would 'speak with new tongues' (Mk 16.17). In Acts 2.4, we read that on the Day of Pentecost the 120 who were gathered in the upper room 'began to speak in other tongues as the Spirit gave them utterance'. Acts 2 is the only example in the New Testament where speaking in other tongues refers to clearly discernible human languages. They were languages not learned by the speaker but were recognizable by many within the audience.

Jordan Daniel May has done an outstanding job of collecting and verifying instances of speaking or praying in 'other tongues' which are in real, authentic languages. These wonderful accounts of supernatural manifestations of the Holy Spirit will inspire and encourage both the preacher and the seeker.

Dr George O. Wood
General Superintendent
General Council of the Assemblies of God

PREFACE

The idea for a book like this came to me in the fall of 2010. Initially, I struggled with the thought. Although a collection of testimonies of 'other tongues' recognized as a human language(s) is certainly worthwhile, this does not represent the type of writing I usually do.

So I prayed but could not shake the idea. After a few weeks, I made a 'deal' with God. I said, 'Lord, I know of two testimonies where someone recognized the actual language spoken when someone prayed in tongues. If I contact both men, and they agree to allow me to publish their stories, then I will know you want me write this book'.

The next week, I contacted Charity Harris, a missionary I had heard while attending Bethel Assembly of God, Jacksonville, NC. There he told an incredible testimony of hearing 300 African believers speak in tongues when baptized in the Holy Spirit. Some were even praising God in English. I asked Brother Charity if I could publish his testimony, and he graciously agreed.

Then I contacted Dr Gary Royer, a missionary and professor under whom I had studied while attending Southwestern Assemblies of God University. He told a story where he heard a young Argentine girl speak in Portuguese when speaking in tongues. She prophesied concerning the soon-coming revival that swept over Argentina winning millions to the Lord. Dr Royer had been a missionary to Brazil, so he easily recognized the language she spoke. I asked Dr Royer if I could publish this story, and like Brother Charity, he graciously agreed.

So as promised, I told the Lord I would write the book. Before I could write, however, I had to collect some testimonies, similar to ones already mentioned. I sent emails to everyone I could find, whether they were Assemblies of God or not. I asked for their testimonies, including:

1. Context (who, when, where)
2. Language spoken and content
3. Outcome (salvation, Spirit-baptism, healing, encouragement, prophecy, etc.)

I started to receive many testimonies. But even those who had no story to share offered words of encouragement. Most told me the project was in their prayers, and many thanked me for writing such a book.

Once collected, I attempted to verify each testimony with more than one witness (when feasible). It was my desire to have as many sources per testimony as possible. Sometimes I received multiple witnesses, yet I still was unable to reach all persons involved (or a relative, if deceased). In these cases, I used either first names only or a generic description (young woman, gentleman, etc.). Those testimonies I was able to verify, I included. If I was unable to confirm a testimony, then it was eliminated. Put plainly, if I had a doubt, I left it out. In the end, I can honestly say I did my best to verify each story.

Nevertheless, I realize that *no amount* of documentation will satisfy a critic. Regardless of the circumstances or any corroborating details, skeptics will *never believe* testimonies like some of those recorded in this book. In their minds, it is impossible for someone to speak in a language they have never learned, since that would be a miracle. And miracles do not happen, according to some. Or, at least, they do not happen today.

But I am a Pentecostal. I believe the Bible when it declares, 'Jesus Christ *is* the same yesterday, today, and forever' (Heb. 13.8). I believe the same God who did wonders and miracles in the past still does them today. After reading this book, perhaps you will too.

INTRODUCTION

Miracles happen! They really do. All over the globe, the Spirit of God touches people in mighty ways. People are delivered from affliction and healed of every kind of disease. They see visions and dream dreams, and even speak in 'other tongues'.

Yes, many Spirit-filled Christians are even speaking in tongues. That is what this book is about. It is a collection of testimonies regarding the miracle of speaking in tongues. Yet this book does not just tell stories, it also bears witness to the fact those who speak in tongues are actually speaking in real, authentic languages. And that is a miracle.

But the greater miracle involves the source of tongues. The Bible tells us that before Jesus ascended, he promised his disciples, 'you shall be baptized with the Holy Spirit not many days from now ... you shall receive power when the Holy Spirit has come upon you; and you shall be witnesses to Me' (Acts 1.5-8). Then on the Day of Pentecost the disciples were *'filled with the Holy Spirit* and began to speak with other tongues, *as the Spirit gave them utterance'* (Acts 2.4, emphasis added). The greater miracle is not the 'other tongues', which simply accompanies the baptism in the Holy Spirit, but rather the fullness of the Holy Spirit residing within an individual believer in a new, mighty way, giving him or her power to be an effective witness for Jesus Christ.

That is the miracle of Pentecost! It is not a dogma or creed. It is not a denomination or movement. It is not even an event or experience. No, it is the anointing of God for effective witness. That is what the baptism in the Holy Spirit is all about. All born-again believers have the Spirit dwelling within them (Jn 3.3-7; Rom. 8.9), but the baptism in the Holy Spirit is a second, subsequent work where the believer is filled with the Spirit of God, or as the resurrected Christ put it, 'endued with power from on high' (Lk. 24.49). That is what the early church had. That is what those who attended the Azusa Street Revival had. And that is what we need today!

Millions of believers have sought the power of the Holy Spirit and yes, they have experienced speaking in tongues. Based on the pattern in Acts, Pentecostals believe speaking in tongues is the 'initial evidence' that a believer has received the baptism in the Holy Spirit. In three out of five biblical accounts, the text explicitly mentions tongues. The first instance occurred when the disciples received the baptism in the Holy Spirit on the Day of Pentecost:

> And suddenly there came a sound from heaven, as of a rushing mighty wind, and it filled the whole house where they were sitting. Then there appeared to them divided tongues, as of fire, and *one* sat upon each of them. And they were all filled with the Holy Spirit and began to speak with other tongues, as the Spirit gave them utterance (Acts 2.2-4).

The second occurred while Peter preached in Caesarea to Cornelius and his household:

> While Peter was still speaking these words, the Holy Spirit fell upon all those who heard the word. And those of the circumcision who believed were astonished, as many as came with Peter, because the gift of the Holy Spirit had been poured out on the Gentiles also. For they heard them speak with tongues and magnify God (Acts 10.44-46).

And the third happened when Paul met some disciples in Ephesus:

> And when Paul had laid hands on them, the Holy Spirit came upon them, and they spoke with tongues and prophesied (Acts 19.6).

By comparing the three accounts, we see only the manifestation of tongues mentioned repeatedly. Other miracles occur (prophecy, rushing mighty wind, etc.), but only speaking in tongues is mentioned in all three accounts, with one affirming tongues as the demonstrable, audible proof the baptism in the Holy Spirit was received: '... For they heard them speak with tongues and magnify God' (10.46).

In the other two recorded Spirit-baptisms, speaking in tongues is either implied in the text or mentioned elsewhere in Scripture. In the case of the Samaritans, an onlooker named Simon 'saw' the Spirit was given by the laying on of hands and offers money for the 'power' to impart the Spirit:

> Now when the apostles who were at Jerusalem heard that Samaria had received the word of God, they sent Peter and John to them, who, when they had come down, prayed for them that they might receive the Holy Spirit. For as yet He had fallen upon none of them. They had only been baptized in the name of the Lord Jesus. Then they laid hands on them, and they received the Holy Spirit. And when Simon saw that through the laying on of the apostles' hands the Holy Spirit was given, he offered them money, saying, 'Give me this power also, that anyone on whom I lay hands may receive the Holy Spirit' (Acts 8.14-19).

Clearly, Simon witnessed something miraculous. Based on the other accounts, it most likely was tongues. In Paul's case, there is no mentioning of tongues (Acts 9.1-20), but Paul himself tells us:

> I thank my God I speak with tongues more than you all ... (1 Cor. 14.18).

When we look at all five accounts, the facts support speaking in tongues as the initial evidence of receiving the baptism in the Holy Spirit.

Once the baptism in the Holy Spirit is received, all Spirit-filled believers can – at the Spirit's prompting – either pray or sing in tongues in daily life for their own spiritual edification (1 Cor. 14.4). Sometimes the Bible calls this praying or singing 'in the Spirit'. But this is distinct from the gift of tongues, when a believer gives a Spirit-inspired 'message in tongues' to the church (corporate body), which is then followed by a Spirit-inspired interpretation. This gift is discussed in great detail in 1 Corinthians 12–14. There the Apostle mentions 'varieties of gifts' given for the 'profit *of all*', or as one translation puts it, the 'common good' (12.7 NASB). In this context, the Spirit gives the gift of tongues for the edification of the whole church. Evidently, some Corinthians were speaking in tongues without an interpretation, which as Paul makes clear, may edify the individual believer but has no benefit for the church (14.1-5). The distinction here is between the *public use* of tongues, which always requires an interpretation, and the *individual use* of tongues for personal, spiritual edification. Paul says, 'If there is no interpreter, [the one speaking in tongues] must keep silent in the church, and speak to himself and God' (14.28). But if there is an interpreter, tongues are permissible since the 'church will be edified' (14.5). Any Spirit-filled believer can speak in tongues for his or her own edification – 'to himself and God' – but not all will manifest the gift of tongues given to edify the church (12.30).

In the following pages, you will find incredible testimonies of both uses of tongues (and even some that do not fit so neatly into either use!). The added twist to these stories, however, is that witnesses actually recognized the tongues as human languages. Some witnesses repented and gave their hearts to the Lord. Many were encouraged and refreshed. But all, like the onlookers on the Day of Pentecost, were amazed by what they heard.

In the end, my hope is that this book will rekindle a fresh desire in the hearts and minds of a young Pentecostal generation; but not just a desire for tongues, as wonderful as that experience is, but a desire for the authentic, mighty baptism in the Holy Spirit.

TESTIMONIES

APACHE

Am I Really Hearing This?

Language: Western Apache (White Mountain dialect)
Location: Prescott, AZ
Date: Summer 2010

At a youth camp in Arizona, a group of Apache Christians prayed with a young Caucasian as he sought fervently the baptism in the Holy Spirit. Suddenly the teenager burst forth in tongues. One of the Apaches, Youth Pastor Chiefo Parker, heard the boy exclaim, *'Bik'ehgo'ihi'dan' Gozho,o,ne'* ('God is good') in the Apache language. The teenager repeated the phrase numerous times.

Shocked by the utterance, Chiefo thought to himself, 'Am I really hearing this? Is this kid really speaking Apache?' Realizing the importance of what just happened, Chiefo ran to the camp's director, missionary Steve Shoop, and the Arizona District Youth Director, Tim Black, to tell them the incredible story of how God had filled the young teenager with the Holy Spirit.

Everyone rejoiced at the glorious news. What happened at the Arizona youth camp was truly a miracle from God.

Sources:

Timothy Black, District Youth Director, Arizona District of the Assemblies of God.

Chiefo Parker, Youth Pastor, Whiteriver Assembly of God, Whiteriver, AZ.

Steve Shoop, Assemblies of God World Missions.

ARABIC

Isa

Language: Arabic
Location: Middle East
Date: Late-60s

Several years ago, missionary Jim Roane experienced great intensity while praying. He prayed in tongues fervently, believing the Lord was having him to intercede for something special. He prayed at every opportunity and noticed he uttered one word repeatedly. The word was *'Isa'*.

Jim and his wife, Bonnie, were puzzled since they had no idea what *'Isa'* meant. Finally, Jim settled on the thought it was the name 'Esau', thinking perhaps he was praying for Esau's descendants somewhere in the Middle East. After some research though, he learned the Babylonians had wiped out Esau's descendants. So he just continued to pray.

Eventually, after the Assemblies of God appointed him as a missionary to the Middle East, Jim discovered the Muslim name for Jesus in Arabic is actually *'Isa'*. The whole time he was simply calling on the name of the Lord.

Source:

Jim and Bonnie Roane, Assemblies of God World Missions.

School of the Spirit

> Language: Arabic (Chadian dialect)
> Location: Rumford, ME
> Date: April 2009

Members of the Praise Assembly of God were in for quite a lesson one Sunday. The Sunday School class focused on the gifts of the Spirit, yet the Spirit was present for more than an academic discussion. In the worship service that morning, a woman named Debra Brown stood and uttered a message in tongues to the congregation. Pastor Justin Thacker almost immediately interpreted: 'True love for God is manifested through a life of worship and praise'. The Spirit's presence filled the congregation as they continued to worship and glorify the name of Jesus.

The gifts of tongues and interpretation are a common occurrence at Praise Assembly, but this particular case was different. Present in the congregation that morning was missionary David Faris, who was home from Chad on furlough. When it came time for him to speak, he approached the pulpit bursting with excitement. He told the congregation the tongue uttered that morning was actually Chadian Arabic. He also confirmed for the congregation that the interpretation was accurate.

Neither Debra Brown nor the Pastor Thacker knew anything of Chadian Arabic, so this was an undeniable, authentic miracle. God was with the congregation. The miracle not only inspired Sister Brown and Pastor Thacker, but it also proved to everyone that the gifts of the Spirit are for today.

Sources:

Debra Brown, Bethel, ME.

David Faris, Assemblies of God World Missions.

Justin Thacker, Pastor, Praise Assembly of God, Rumford, ME.

He Spoke in Upper Egyptian Arabic

Language: Arabic (Upper Egyptian dialect)
Location: St. Paul, MN
Date: Mid-1980s

During a Sunday morning service at Summit Avenue Assembly of God (later Summit Church), Hugh Robinson uttered a message in tongues. After a few moments, a choir member – Carl Thompson, a Gideon who later became a Trustee for the International Gideon Cabinet – gave the interpretation. The message was an uplifting, encouraging word for the congregation.

In attendance was David Irwin, long-time missionary to Egypt and former international coordinator for the Center for Ministry to Muslims. After the service, he asked both men if either knew Arabic. But Hugh and Carl had no idea what he was talking about.

By this time, Pastor Ed Tedeschi walked over to join the conversation. Brother Irwin then told the guys something incredible. He informed everyone that Hugh's message was actually in Upper Egyptian Arabic, the specific dialect from the area of Egypt where he served, and Carl's interpretation was completely accurate. When they heard the news, both Hugh and Carl replied, 'Praise the Lord'.

Sources:

Paul Irwin, Pastor of Marriage and Counseling, National Community Church, Washington, DC. Paul is the son of the late David Irwin. He was Pastor Tedeschi's associate at the time of this story.

Ed Tedeschi, Assistant Superintendent, Minnesota District of the Assemblies of God.

Charlotte Thompson, St. Paul, MN. Charlotte is the wife of the late Carl Thompson.

The Lord's Prayer

Language: Arabic
Location: Dallas, TX
Date: 1986

While attending Christ for the Nations Institute (CFNI), Sharon Reeves had a Palestinian roommate named Elizabeth. One morning, they both went to pray in the CFNI prayer room. It was a little crowded, so they knelt down on different sides of the room.

After a few minutes, Elizabeth rushed over to Sharon shaking with excitement. 'A young woman just prayed the Lord's Prayer next to me in perfect Arabic', she exclaimed. Yet when they asked the young woman if she spoke Arabic, she did not know a word.

This amazing experience had an enormous impact on Elizabeth, who was feeling depressed. She was away from home for the first time, but God, through the Arabic prayer, gave her a great sense of peace, confirming his presence with her.

Source:

Sharon Reeves, Assemblies of God World Missions.

CREOLE

That's God!

Language: Creole (Haitian dialect)
Location: Paris, Ontario
Date: July 1998

At a youth meeting at Braeside Camp, Mark Griffin – who served as the DYD (District Youth Director) for the Pentecostal Assemblies of Canada in the Western Ontario District – asked a young man who was seeking prayer, 'What can I pray for?'

'God knows ... so whatever is fine', he responded. Mark waited a moment but received no clear direction from the Spirit. So he whispered a prayer in tongues.

After a minute, Mark said, 'Are you sure there isn't anything for me to pray about?'

'No, that's perfect', the young man replied. 'The part you prayed about my family – that was right on! That was a great encouragement to me. Thank you ... thank you. Oh, and by the way, your Creole is excellent. Have you spent time in Haiti?'

Mark was stunned. 'I don't speak Creole', he responded.

The young man laughed. 'Come on, even your accent is perfect', he said. 'I'd swear you were born there!'

Mark insisted he could not speak Creole. He explained he was simply speaking in tongues.

'Oh yeah, I've heard people in my church do that before', said the young man. 'But I didn't know it could be in Creole ... that's cool. I just got back after six months in Haiti and I never expected someone to pray for me tonight in Creole. That's GOD ... THAT'S GOD!'

Source:

D. Mark Griffin, Pentecostal Assemblies of Canada International Missionary.

ET ASI

Language: Creole (Haitian dialect)
Location: Brantford, Ontario
Date: March 25, 2008

Dave Carrol is one of the pastors at Freedom House in Brantford, Ontario. Every Tuesday evening, he leads a small group focused on intercessory prayer. During one of the meetings, he started praying in tongues.

After his prayer, a new attendee named Erica asked if he knew what he was saying. Confused at first, Dave thought of the Apostle Paul's words: 'In the same way the Spirit also helps our weakness; for we do not know how to pray as we should, but the Spirit Himself intercedes for us with groanings too deep for words; and He who searches the hearts knows what the mind of the Spirit is, because He intercedes for the saints according to the will of God' (Rom. 8.26-27 NASB).

But Erica was not referencing Romans. No, she actually understood part of Dave's prayer. When praying, he repeatedly uttered, *'Et asi'*, which is Creole for, 'As it's written'. Erica moved around a lot as a child and lived in Haiti for a time. Hearing Dave's prayer reminded her of when Haitian Christians would say, *'Et asi'*, and then, 'Amen', meaning, 'As it's written … so be it'.

As Erica spoke, Dave recalled when he initially received the baptism in the Holy Spirit. His pastor's wife, Andrea, had prayed over him at an altar, encouraging him just to let God speak through him. When he fully surrendered to God, words like *'Et asi'* began to flow out of his mouth.

Sources:

Erica Akers, Ancaster, Ontario.

Dave Carrol, Youth and Young Adults Pastor, Freedom House, Brantford, Ontario.

ENGLISH

It Was Funny!

Language: English
Location: Cochabamba, Bolivia
Date: November 2004

Something funny happened in 2004 at the Bolivian General Council of the Assemblies of God. During one of the altar services, the Holy Spirit moved upon a young woman in such a way that she started to laugh uncontrollably. In this time of 'Holy Laughter', the young woman began speaking in English, 'It's so humorous! God, I didn't know you were so humorous!'

Dr Joseph Castleberry, longtime missionary to Bolivia and Ivy League-trained educator, was amazed by this. He approached the woman and to his surprise, she could not speak English. She did not know what she was saying, since she was speaking in tongues. So Dr Castleberry translated. Her response was almost as unusual as the event itself. She responded, *'Pues, si fue bien comico'* ('Well, it WAS funny!').

Source:

Dr Joseph Castleberry, President, Northwest University (Assemblies of God), Kirkland, WA.

Surrounded by Angels

Language: English
Location: Kyoto, Japan
Date: 1921

John and Margaret Gaines were not on the mission field long before life's trials began to weigh on their souls. Margaret and her baby boy, Paul, were terribly sick and John started to wonder if they needed to return to America. So John prayed earnestly, 'Heavenly Father, am I in the right place, or should I take my family to safety? I want to do your will above all things, but I need confirmation'.

Soon after, the couple held a service in Kyoto. When John gave the altar call, an elderly Japanese woman came forward. She knelt and prayed silently for nearly two hours. Finally, the woman lifted her hands and began praising God aloud. She stood up and walked around the church, repeating the English phrase, 'I'm surrounded by angels'.

When the woman stopped, John asked her where she learned English. The woman was confused. 'I don't know English … I barely know my own language', she said in Japanese. 'Since I was a child, I've walked by here on my way to the Shinto Shrine to pray. But today I was so tired and cold. Since there is a welcome sign on your door, I decided to come in to get warm. The music was so pleasing and the message assured me Jesus would receive me. I prayed and Jesus answered my prayer. He saved me. In 68 years, Shinto never answered me'.

Amazed by the woman's utterance, John knew then that the Lord had answered his prayer with a powerful confirmation.

Source:

Margaret H. Gaines, Church of God World Missions (retired). The couple in this story (John Wesley Gaines and Margaret

Faith Piper Gaines) were the parents of Margaret H. Gaines. John told this story to his daughter, Margaret, before she went to the mission field in North Africa. He did so only after he realized she would not be dissuaded from going to North Africa alone at the age of 20.

Oh, the Grace of the Lord!

Language: English (but with a Chinese accent)
Location: Kaohsiung City, Taiwan
Date: Mid-1950s

A young Taiwanese man's family became outraged when he converted to Christ. He tried explaining the gospel to them, but they simply would not listen. As the first-born male, his responsibilities included many of the family's pagan rituals. When he refused to renounce Christ, they began persecuting him.

The next time the young man went to church, he told the missionaries that his parents had beaten him. The message that night was on the baptism in the Holy Spirit, and he was open to receive. A group gathered around and instructed him to focus on Jesus – to yield his voice, lips, and tongue to the Holy Spirit and let him take control. He was timid at first but gradually learned to praise the Lord audibly.

As he yielded to the Spirit, he began making unintelligible sounds. As he continued to worship the Lord, he suddenly broke forth in English. 'Oh the grace of the Lord! Oh the grace of the Lord! Oh the grace of the Lord!' he repeatedly exclaimed (but with a Chinese accent).

The other believers rejoiced, yet only the missionaries understood his tongue as English. It was just a repetition of a few words, but there was great meaning in those few words! God's grace was helping him follow the Lord and endure the persecution from his family. It may sound like gibberish when someone speaks in tongues, but just a few sounds can have an abundance of meaning when spoken by the power of the Spirit!

Source:

Robert and Evelyn Bolton, Assemblies of God World Missions (retired).

Worshiping in Tongues

Language: English
Location: Bangkok, Thailand
Date: 1971

Something amazing happened early in Bruce and Kay Mumm's ministry. As Bruce wrapped up one of his sermons, a local pastor invited those in attendance to come forward for the baptism in the Holy Spirit. Among those who came was an elderly Chinese woman. As she began to worship the Lord, her praise turned into English. She uttered a few short English praises in perfect 'American English'.

Kay was surprised but delighted to know there was another English speaker present. After the service, Kay approached the woman but soon discovered she could not understand a word of English. She was simply worshiping God in tongues the whole time.

Source:

Bruce and Kay Mumm, Assemblies of God World Missions.

Tell All the People

Language: English
Location: Taipei, Taiwan
Date: Fall 1974

Sally Snider served with the Assemblies of God MAPS (Mission America Placement Service) Program in Taipei, Taiwan. One morning, she heard a man praying in English on a lower level of her apartment building.

'Listen!' Sally told a friend, 'someone's praying in English!' The prayer went like this: 'Jesus is Lord! Tell all the people of the world ... Jesus is Lord!' Since Sally believed she was the only Christian living in the building, the prayer surprised her.

Sally soon discovered there was a Christian man living on the second floor though. A few days later, she attempted to speak to him in English, but he just stared at her with a puzzled look. 'No speak English ... no speak English', he said.

Sally was a little confused, since she knew she heard him praying in English just a few days earlier. Then it dawned on Sally. The Christian man was praying in tongues that morning.

Excited at the thought, Sally recalled how a friend tried to convince her that tongues had ceased. Once she realized what happened though, she now had undeniable proof that the miracle of speaking in tongues is for today.

Source:

Brian and Sally Snider, Assemblies of God World Missions.

The Spirit Speaks Texan?

Language: English (but with a south Texas drawl)
Location: Guiglo, Ivory Coast
Date: 1973

Missionaries Willard Teague and Aimé Cizéron experienced great success during an evangelistic rally in Guiglo, a town near the city of Duekoue in the Ivory Coast. The crowds numbered in the thousands and the meetings went on for nights. Before long, however, demonic interference threatened the missionaries' work.

So the two missionaries prayed that the Holy Spirit would block all demonic activity during the preaching. Aimé, a Frenchman, began to pray in English. He thanked the Lord in advance for answering their prayers. Willard was surprised, since he had not heard him speak, much less, pray in English before. What was even more amazing was Aimé spoke with a south Texas drawl! This astonished Willard, a native Texan. When he expressed his surprise at the prayer, Aimé was even more shocked than Willard. He did not know English; he was simply praying in tongues.

Through Aimé's prayer, God assured the missionaries he would empower them to continue proclaiming the gospel, uninterrupted and unhindered by demonic disruption.

Source:

Dr Willard Teague, Dean, Undergraduate School of Bible and Theology, Global University, Springfield, MO.

… Now Just Watch

Language: English
Location: Lomé, Togo
Date: 1994

Missionary Charity Harris was in Lomé, Togo as rebel forces attempted a military coup. In response to the upheaval, the government imposed a strict curfew between the hours of 6.00 pm and 6.00 am. Although the government foiled the coup, they took the threat seriously. Death was the penalty for breaking curfew.

In the middle of the chaos, a local congregation invited Charity to preach one evening. Since the curfew was still in effect, he had to make the tough decision whether to go or not. On top of that, he was recovering from being poisoned by a witch doctor, who mistakenly thought he was with the CIA. Faced with these challenges, Charity still decided to risk the danger and accept the invitation to preach.

That evening the crowd numbered around 300. Charity preached on the Holy Spirit; but when it came time for an altar call, he was simply too weak to pray for the people individually. He leaned against the pulpit, lifted his head towards heaven, and pleaded, 'I simply can't do any more'.

The Lord responded audibly, 'You've done your job … now just watch'. The awesome power of the presence of God then gripped Charity as he looked out over the congregation. Immediately, people on his right began speaking in tongues. Then it started in the center. And then it started on the left. The sounds of Pentecost filled the air. In a matter of seconds, the Lord poured out the Holy Spirit over the entire congregation and they were all speaking in tongues. Charity could hear tongues throughout the entire congregation. He even heard many praising God in perfect English.

Source:

Charity and Ruth Harris, Assemblies of God World Missions (retired). Charity is the founder of Worldwide Good News Crusades, Sand Springs, OK.

Spirit of Thanksgiving

Language: English
Location: Trelew, Argentina
Date: 1996

In 1996, Martin and Charlotte Jacobson, missionaries to Argentina, hosted an AIM (Ambassadors in Missions) team from Kentucky. The team included the then District Superintendent, James Biram. On their first Sunday morning, Superintendent Biram preached at a local church where there was a great move of God. In response to his message, many believers came forward to receive the baptism in the Holy Spirit. The Spirit's presence was so real and powerful that many prayed while lying face down.

After the service, the congregation offered the team lunch in another room. Something unforgettable then happened. A young teenage girl named Julieta rushed into the room and interrupted the team's lunch. Shaking with excitement, the girl testified in English to how God just baptized her in the Holy Spirit. After speaking, she sat down and prayed quietly. The team applauded and then continued to eat.

Before long, Martin, the host missionary, made an incredible announcement. He told the team that the church's pastor, Ramón Saucedo, had just informed him Julieta did not know English. The team was stunned!

Later that night, Martin told the team Julieta had prayed for a way to thank them. Simply trusting the Lord, Julieta entered the room and, by faith, began speaking in tongues. A miracle took place right before the team's eyes that day. Just like on the Day of Pentecost, the team heard Julieta, now filled with the Holy Spirit, speak the wonderful works of God.

Sources:

David and Deborah Amsler, Assemblies of God World Missions. David is the former District Youth Director, Kentucky District of the Assemblies of God.

James Biram, former Superintendent, Kentucky District of the Assemblies of God.

Martin and Charlotte Jacobson, Assemblies of God World Missions. Martin is the Director, Patagonian Bible Institute, Gaiman, Argentina.

Jesus Was There

Language: English
Location: Uige, Angola
Date: 2002

Missionary Mark Gardner travelled to Uige, Northern Angola with a team from Calvary Temple, Wayne, NJ. The trip occurred not long after the conclusion of Angola's civil war. The war-torn country was ripe for harvest.

As part of the trip, Dr Tom Keinath, pastor of Calvary Temple, led a Pastors' School for some of the local pastors. At the conclusion of one of the meetings, an Angolan man, one who did not know English, started speaking in English, 'Jesus is here! Jesus is here! Jesus is here!' The man repeated the phrase several times. The team felt very encouraged. What a miraculous way to conclude a Pastors' School!

When the team returned home, another miracle occurred in Uige. When the deadly Marburg virus broke out, God healed all those infected who visited the church where Pastor Keinath led his Pastors' School. TRULY, JESUS WAS THERE!

Sources:

Mark and Kim Gardner, Assemblies of God World Missions.

Dr Tom Keinath, Pastor, Calvary Temple, Wayne, NJ.

He Opened Her Womb

Language: English
Location: Dapango, Togo
Date: November 1949

Reverends Murray Nelson Brown, Sr. and Marjorie May Brown (née Ball) served as missionaries to West Africa from 1940 to 1980. Not long after arriving in West Africa, they welcomed their first child into this world, a baby girl named Ruth Elaine. Little did they know, however, that a decade would pass before having another child. They prayed endlessly over the years, and yet faced one failed pregnancy after another. They almost gave up, but God would prove to be miraculous.

While serving in Dapango (now Dapaon), Togo, Marjorie overhead an African child praying in English: 'You're going to have another baby, and it will be a boy. When he is born you will know nothing is impossible with God!'

Yet the African child could not speak English; he was praying in tongues. God spoke a prophetic word through the young child specifically for Marjorie – a word not only of encouragement but also of promise.

Murray Nelson Brown, Jr. was Brother and Sister Brown's miracle baby. He was born on September 9, 1950 at the Ridge Hospital in Accra, Ghana. He is now Reverend Brown and serves as the current Executive Director of Teen Challenge, Greater Cleveland, OH.

Source:

Murray N. Brown, Jr., Executive Director of Teen Challenge, Greater Cleveland, OH.

... Would Praise God in English

Language: English (but with a Caribbean accent)
Location: Barcelona, Spain
Date: Between 1989 and 1999

When Craig Mathison served as a missionary to Barcelona, he witnessed something unusual. During several meetings, a Spanish pastor would praise God in English. This happened many times throughout the years.

Craig questioned him at first, but the pastor did not know English. He was simply praying quietly in tongues during the corporate worship. He never intended it as a 'message in tongues'.

The funniest thing about the whole event was the pastor's accent, which was very distinct from how Spaniards typically speak English. He pronounced vowel sounds common to English but unknown in Spanish. The accent with which he spoke actually sounded like someone from the Caribbean.

Source:

Craig Mathison, Lead Netweaver at TEVO (an initiative of the Europe Region of the U.S. Assemblies of God World Missions to connect new resources to the many spiritual needs of Europe).

I Did What You Told Me

Language: English
Location: Malawi
Date: 1963

In the early-1960s, Charity Harris traveled through some Malawian churches promoting the local Assemblies of God Bible Colleges. At one of his meetings, many youth came forward to receive the baptism in the Holy Spirit.

As the youth sought the Lord, Brother Harris heard a young man praising God in perfect English. He watched the young man stand there with hands lifted high, praising God for all of his blessings. Charity was surprised since he thought he was the only English-speaker present.

After the service, Charity approached the young man and spoke to him in English. The young man could not understand a word though. So Charity spoke to him in Chinyaja, the language of Malawi. 'Why were you praying in English?' Charity asked.

'I did what you told me to do', the young man responded. 'I allowed the Holy Spirit to speak through me in any language he wanted to use. And that's what I did'.

Source:

Charity and Ruth Harris, Assemblies of God World Missions (retired). Charity is the founder of Worldwide Good News Crusades, Sand Springs, OK.

Listen to the Vietnamese Man …

Language: English
Location: Somewhere in the Mekong Delta, Vietnam
Date: August 1996

Something miraculous happened when a delegation from the Louisiana District of the Assemblies of God travelled to Vietnam. The team included the former District Superintendent, Lowell Ashbrook, the then DYD (District Youth Director), Gary Sapp, and several other ministers.

When they arrived, the team took boats down the Mekong Delta. The Vietnamese government forced Christians to worship underground, so the group gathered behind a secluded Buddhist temple.

At the conclusion of one of the services, Paul Ai, then the General Superintendent of the Vietnamese Assemblies of God, encouraged everyone to pray in the Spirit. As the ministers prayed, Luke Patrick, one of the Louisiana ministers, nudged Gary Sapp. 'Listen to the Vietnamese man standing beside me', he said. 'He is praising God in perfect English'.

'The man probably knows English', Gary replied. When the prayer concluded, both Gary and Luke asked the Vietnamese man if he knew English. The man just looked at them puzzled. They then called Superintendent Ai over to interpret. When Brother Ai explained to the man what had happened, the man burst forth in praises to God.

Sources:

Paul Ai, President, Vietnamese Outreach International, Hampton, VA.

Luke Patrick, Oak Grove, LA.

Gary Sapp, Missions Representative for Mission of Mercy, Colorado Springs, CO.

She Heard Her Worship in English

Language: English
Location: Pavia, Venezuela
Date: August 2010

In August 2010, missionary Chris Nelson hosted a short-term missions team from Raleigh First Assembly of God. On the first night of services, members of the team walked through the crowd praying for those seeking the baptism in the Holy Spirit.

One of the members named Susan Smith then witnessed something amazing. As she prayed with a woman named Marta Hernandez, she heard her worship the Lord in English. Susan was surprised, since she thought the mission team members were the only ones who could speak English.

After the service, Susan decided to speak with Marta but quickly discovered she could not understand English. What Susan witnessed that day was an authentic miracle from God.

Sources:

Marta Hernandez, Pavia, Venezuela.

Chris and Angela Nelson, Assemblies of God World Missions.

Susan Smith, Raleigh, NC.

Praise Be to Jesus, the Lord

Language: English
Location: Crotone, Italy
Date: 1978

The local Assembly of God church in Crotone, a small town in southern Italy, invited missionary Terry Peretti to preach a week-long revival. During one of the services, he invited the youth to the altar to seek the baptism in the Holy Spirit. About 20 came forward for prayer.

Terry moved through the crowd, praying and laying hands on each one. One young man then suddenly lifted his hands and began praising God in English. 'Thank you, Lord! Praise be to Jesus, the Lord!' he repeated.

Terry thought the young man must have studied English at the university. After asking him, however, he discovered he had just received the baptism in the Holy Spirit. He was simply praising the Lord in tongues.

Source:

Terry and Marsha Peretti, Assemblies of God World Missions.

Open Your Mouth and Praise the Lord

Language: English
Location: Cali, Columbia
Date: 1967

Paul Brannen's father, Bill, came to visit him while he pastored one of the local churches in Cali, Columbia. Bill pastored in Maysville, KY and wanted to preach a revival in Columbia. He had hoped to bring back exciting stories and reports of large crowds to his congregation in Kentucky.

On the first night, Bill issued an invitation through Paul, who acted as his interpreter, 'Everyone who needs the baptism in the Holy Spirit, come down to the altar and we will pray with you until you receive'. Practically everyone rushed to the altar. Unfortunately, they had little success that night.

The next night, Bill preached on receiving the baptism in the Holy Spirit by the laying on of hands. When he gave the invitation, once again nearly everyone came forward. Many received this time, but there was one faithful church worker named Oscar who did not. Night after night, Oscar came forward but with no success.

On the last night, Oscar, who now felt a bit discouraged, came forward to the altar again. Bill gave verbal instruction to those at the altar and, though none understood English, they did exactly what he directed them to do. Bill approached Oscar and said, 'Brother, lift up your hands'. Oscar, who did not know English, obeyed and lifted his hands. 'Raise your head up', said Bill. So Oscar did. Bill continued, 'Now open your mouth and praise the Lord'. What happened next surprised both Bill and Paul. Oscar opened his mouth and began praising God in perfect English!

Source:

Paul and Betty Brannan, Assemblies of God World Missions. Paul is the resource editor for the Missions Awareness Team (Assemblies of God).

Praising God and Giving Thanks

Language: English
Location: Megrine, Tunisia
Date: 1954

When missionary Margaret Gaines served in Tunisia, she utilized a small three-room garage as a church. There in the shadow of a Roman Catholic Cathedral, Margaret experienced mighty moves of the Spirit. During one of her services, believers crammed into one of the rooms and fervently worshiped the Lord.

Suddenly the Holy Spirit filled the entire room. The power was so intense Margaret collapsed on the floor, blinded by a vision of glory. When her sight returned, she heard three people praying in tongues. One was even speaking in perfect English, praising God and giving thanks for the Holy Spirit. Sister Margaret was truly amazed, knowing she was the only English-speaker present.

Source:

Margaret H. Gaines, Church of God World Missions (retired). Also, see Margaret Gaines, *Of Like Passions: Missionary to the Arabs* (Cleveland, TN: Pathway, 2000), p. 122.

Spoken in Perfect English

Language: English
Location: Burkino Faso
Date: 1965

A great revival swept over Burkina Faso in 1965. Many accepted Christ and more than 2,000 believers received the baptism in the Holy Spirit.

During one of the services, a young man named Teedawendy from the Bible School of Nagabangre, where the revival started, spoke in perfect English when baptized in the Holy Spirit. Yet Teedawendy did not know English, and he lived hundreds of miles from any English speakers. Several professors witnessed this miracle, including Sidibe Zabre, Moussa Rapadamnaba, and the American missionary, Dr Del Tarr. After praying in tongues, Teedawendy could not even make a simple greeting in English.

Source:

Dr Del Tarr, Missions Pastor, Capital Christian Center, Sacramento, CA, and former President and Professor Emeritus, Assemblies of God Theological Seminary, Springfield, MO. Also, see Del Tarr, *The Foolishness of God: A Linguist Looks at the Mystery of Tongues* (Springfield, MO: Access, 2010), p. 401.

Strange Words in Your Mind

Language: English (but with a California accent)
Locations: Mendoza Province, Argentina
Date: 1966

Night after night, Ralph Hiatt prayed for the Lord to pour out the Holy Spirit as he held youth meetings in western Argentina. One night, as the youth prayed up front, it seemed like wave upon wave of the Holy Spirit swept over them. The praise would rise to a crescendo and then subside, yet no one spoke in tongues.

As Ralph prayed on the platform, he sensed the Holy Spirit directing him to stop the prayer for a moment and give an explanation. He believed the Lord wanted him to announce that the Holy Spirit sometimes places foreign words in our minds. Ralph, not wanting to deprive the youth of a genuine experience, argued with the Lord. He never gave such an explanation before or even heard of such a thing.

Finally, after struggling with the Lord for almost an hour, Ralph stopped the prayer. He told the youth, 'The Holy Spirit doesn't bypass our intellects. Sometimes he puts new words in our minds. It's then up to us to speak them out in praise to God. We are now going to pray again. This time, when the power of the Spirit flows over us, be ready to praise the Lord with the strange words the Holy Spirit puts in our minds'.

The group started to pray again as Ralph went to the corner of the platform. Suddenly he began to fear his explanation might rob someone of an authentic spiritual experience. Ralph wept at the thought. He only desired the genuine experience of the baptism in the Holy Spirit for the youth.

Then he had an idea. 'Lord when you baptize somebody, have them speak in English', he prayed. 'Then I'll know it's real.'

Another wave of Holy Spirit swept over the group. As Ralph looked into the crowd, he saw one of the local ministers, Pastor

Ernesto Coronel, standing in the middle of the group. With a big grin on his face, he stood there and pointed to an 18-year old girl.

Ralph rushed to the front of the platform, hoping to hear someone finally speaking in tongues. The girl was only about four feet in front of him. He could not believe what he was hearing. She was speaking in perfect California English. 'Praise your name! Praise your name!' she repeated.

Ralph jumped off the platform and asked the pastor if the girl knew English. The pastor said she was an uneducated field worker who had no contact with English speakers. 'But she's speaking in English', Ralph shouted.

'Are you sure?' Pastor Coronel asked.

'Of course I'm sure', Ralph responded. 'Every word is clear'. It was only three words but it was truly miraculous. For nearly half an hour the girl repeated the same phrase over and over again.

Later that night, Ralph asked her if she knew English, but she assured him she did not. When Ralph told her what happened, the young woman was truly amazed.

Sources:

Doyle Jones, *Be Filled with the Spirit: Powerful, Life-Changing Instructions for a Spirit-Filled Life* (Mustang, OK: Tate, 2006), p. 54.

Ralph Hiatt, Assemblies of God World Missions (retired).

I've Got It, I've Got It

Language: English
Location: Guatemala
Date: 1967

Before James Allen served as Secretary/Treasurer for the Louisiana District of the Assemblies of God, he and his wife, Juanita, traveled to Guatemala for a short-term missions trip. During one of the services, Juanita prayed with a Guatemalan teenage girl who had sought the baptism in the Holy Spirit for some time.

Suddenly the Lord filled the teenage girl with the Spirit and she began speaking in tongues. Yet her tongue was actually English. By the power of the Spirit, she uttered, 'I've got it! I've got it! Praise God ... I've got it!' Apparently, she was so overjoyed that her spirit erupted within her with praise for the Lord's blessing.

Source:

Michael and Marigold Cheshier, Assemblies of God Evangelists/Missionaries, Springfield, MO. Juanita Allen was the mother of Marigold.

... that Beautifully and Intimately

Language: English
Location: Temuco, Chile
Date: 1978

Glen and Sharon Pummel served as Foursquare missionaries to Chile from 1975 to 1983. On one occasion, when preaching in Temuco, something miraculous happened. As they prayed for about 20 believers to receive the baptism in the Holy Spirit, one woman began praising and worshiping Jesus in perfect English.

The woman's utterance surprised Glen, since he knew she did not know English. 'I wish I'd praise Jesus that beautifully and intimately', he thought to himself.

Source:

Glen Pummel, District Administrator and Missions Director, MidSouth District, Foursquare Church.

Thank You, Jesus

Language: English
Location: Dakar, Senegal
Date: 2000

During an altar call at Temple Evangelique in Senegal, a young woman suddenly started screaming. Everyone around her was startled at first, but many began praying. Eventually she calmed down and started worshiping the Lord in clear English. 'Thank you, Jesus! I praise you, Jesus!' she uttered repeatedly.

After the service, Vern and Janice Finck, then missionaries to Senegal, talked with the young woman. Vern asked her in English, 'What was happening when you screamed?' The young woman just looked confused and began speaking on another subject in French. He again spoke to her in English and again she ignored his question.

Standing nearby was a young man. 'Pastor Vern, you have to speak in French. She doesn't speak English', he said.

'Oh yes, she does', Vern replied. 'She was worshiping the Lord in English earlier'. The young man did not believe it, so Vern asked the woman in French if she spoke English.

'No', she replied in French, 'I don't speak English'.

Later, Vern returned to the subject of why the young woman screamed. She replied, 'Evil spirits where attacking me. But at the altar, I saw what appeared to be a snake slithering toward me. When I screamed though, I saw a heel twist down on its head, killing it instantly'.

Source:

Vern and Janice Finck, Assemblies of God World Missions.

ESTONIAN

Who's that Man?

Language: Estonian
Location: Columbus, OH
Date: 1960

One Saturday night, the Lord prompted Pastor Don Neel to get out of bed. The Spirit said, 'Find a man ... he needs Jesus'.

Pastor Neel left his house at midnight and started driving around. Arriving near a shopping center, he noticed someone who looked depressed walking across the parking lot. He drove up and asked the man to get in. His name was Mr. Jones. 'How are you and Jesus getting along?' Pastor Neel asked.

Dropping his head, he whimpered, 'Not very well'. Mr. Jones told Pastor Neel he was backslidden. They talked for a while and then Pastor Neel drove a few blocks to Fairmore Assembly of God (later named Evangel Temple). There Mr. Jones recommitted his life to the Lord.

Two weeks later, Mr. Jones gave a message in tongues at Fairmore Assembly. No interpretation followed, but present in the congregation were the Kleemans, a young Lutheran couple from Estonia. Having both Mr. and Mrs. Kleeman in attendance was unusual, since Mr. Kleeman, who had difficulty believing in tongues, typically waited in the car. Yet this Sunday he finally decided to come in and was surprised by what he heard Mr. Jones utter.

Later, Mr. Kleeman called Pastor Neel and asked, 'Who's the man who spoke my language?' Pastor Neel was stunned, but explained to him that Mr. Jones was actually speaking in tongues.

Pastor Neel's answer surprised Mr. Kleeman, who never revealed the content of Mr. Jones' message. Yet evidently, it was exactly what he needed to hear; Mr. Kleeman never missed another service.

Source:

Don and Sophia Neel, retired Assemblies of God pastors, New Iberia, LA.

FARSI

One Sunday Morning

Language: Farsi (Persian)
Location: Marshall, WA
Date: 1978

A group of college students attended Marshall Community Church one Sunday morning. One of the students invited an Iranian Muslim student to visit with them. During the service, a church member near the students began speaking in tongues. The gifts of the Spirit were commonplace at Marshall Community, but no one knew exactly how the Iranian visitor would respond.

What they would soon find out was shocking though. While the students heard the member praising God in 'other tongues', the Iranian visitor actually heard his native language. He later told the students that the member was praising God in perfect Farsi, the official language of Iran. The students explained speaking in tongues to him, but he was still surprised. Like the witnesses on the Day of Pentecost, he wondered how he could hear someone speak his native language.

The Iranian visitor did not convert that morning, but it was undeniable to him and everyone else that God's presence was in Marshall Community Church that morning.

Source:

Tom Isenhart, Foursquare Relief and Compassion and Pastor Emeritus, Puget Sound Christian Center, Tacoma, WA.

FRENCH

You're Speaking French!

Language: French
Location: Cincinnati, OH
Date: Spring 1980

In the spring of 1980, many students gave their lives to Christ during a mini-revival at the University of Cincinnati. Bill Shrader was one of them. Each night of the revival, a group of students would gather in a dorm room and pray from about 11.00 pm to 1.00 am.

On April 8, 1980, two students invited Bill to pray. They met in a dorm room and as they prayed, the other students, Scott and David, started speaking in tongues. Bill was truly amazed. He had read about tongues in the Bible, but never actually witnessed it.

Since Bill was eager for every blessing God was giving, he asked Scott and Dave if they would pray for him to receive the baptism in the Holy Spirit. As they laid their hands on his shoulders and prayed, he began to feel his upper pallet wanting to lift. 'If I make any noise right now, it'll sound French', he thought to himself. He was a little embarrassed, since Dave and Scott did not sound French when speaking in tongues.

But Bill's desire was great, so he added sound to the feeling in the back of his throat and began to speak. David and Scott looked at him with great joy. 'You're speaking French!' they exclaimed.

Overwhelmed with excitement, Bill went to bed knowing his life would never be the same again. That night, he even woke up speaking in tongues in his sleep.

Source:

Bill and Lena Shrader, Assemblies of God World Missions.

More of You, God

Language: French
Location: Woodworth, LA
Date: July 2000

Two Belgium students volunteered at the Louisiana Kids' Camp one summer. As they sat on the front row, they observed two kids praying, facing each other. After listening to what they were saying, the students realized the two kids were actually speaking French to each other, conversing in a prayer to God. One of the kids prayed, *'Plus de vous, Dieu! Je veux plus de toi!'* ('More of you, God! I want more of you!'). The other kid echoed affirmatively, *'Oui Dieu, plus!'* ('Yes God, more!'). But neither child knew French, they were simply praying in the Spirit.

Source:

Hutson L. Goza, Jr., Secretary/Treasurer, Louisiana District of the Assemblies of God.

Trust Your Heart, not Your Head

Language: French
Location: Cincinnati, OH
Date: 1981

Shortly after Bill Shrader received the baptism in the Holy Spirit, he went to Sunday morning service at First Christian Assembly of God, Cincinnati, OH. During the service, the pastor asked those with prayer needs to raise their hands. Bill saw a woman on the other side of the church with her hand raised high, so he went over and joined the small group praying for her. By coincidence, he just happened to be in front of her, with his hand on her shoulder. He started praying in tongues and she looked up at him, startled.

'Do you speak French?' she probed.

'No', he replied.

So she asked, 'Do you know what you just prayed?'

Again, he said, 'No'.

She continued, 'I raised my hand because I need God's help in making a decision. And you just said, "Trust your heart, not your head"'.

With no idea what to pray about, Bill trusted the Holy Spirit to give him the exact words at the right time to utter.

Source:

Bill and Lena Shrader, Assemblies of God World Missions.

Do You Remember I Speak French?

Language: French
Location: Dayton, OH
Date: February 2011

Over the years, many have interpreted Bill Shrader's prayer language as French. When it happens though, it is usually not a Parisian accent. Rather it appears to be most frequently a North African dialect. Twice, missionaries from North Africa have recognized his tongue.

The most recent case involves a friend of Bill's, who attended a Chi Alpha meeting at Wright State University. While kneeling at the altar, Bill prayed in tongues. His friend looked up and asked, 'Do you remember I speak French?' as if to say, 'Hey, I know what you're praying about'.

Bill just continued to pray. His friend later confirmed their prayers were in agreement.

Source:

Bill and Lena Shrader, Assemblies of God World Missions.

GERMAN

Be Open to the Holy Spirit

Language: German
Location: North Myrtle Beach, SC
Date: June 1974

In the early-1970s, the Lord placed a heavy burden for the lost on the hearts of Richard Taylor and group of young people from Rock Hill First Assembly of God. Hearing of the rampant sin on the beaches, they decided to travel to North Myrtle Beach to start a summer ministry named 'Operation Beachhead'.

Summer after summer, they saw thousands come to Lord. A typical day included prayer in the morning, witnessing during the day, and an evening baptism in the Atlantic Ocean.

One evening, Larry Boan, who was the youth pastor at Rock Hill First Assembly, went to the beach to evangelize. While sharing tracts, he saw a young man walking. 'Hey buddy, where're you headed?' Larry yelled out.

'To the pier', the man replied.

'No, where're you headed when you die?' Larry clarified.

The young man stopped as Larry shared the gospel with him. The man's name was Bob and after listening to Larry, he repented and confessed Christ as Lord and Savior.

Larry then invited Bob back to the Operation Beachhead residence. There he provided Bob with some Christian literature and invited him to the evening water baptism. As they walked back to the beach, Larry encouraged Bob to be open to the Holy Spirit (though he did not mention tongues). After they arrived,

Larry began baptizing the new believers in the Atlantic. When it was Bob's turn, he went down into the water but quickly shot up with his hands raised high, speaking loudly in tongues.

As Richard Taylor watched from the beach, a stranger, whose name was David they later learned, paced back and forth behind him. When Bob arose from the water speaking in tongues, David began asking questions. Yet Richard said he did not know anything about Bob, except that he just became a Christian.

What happened next surprised Richard. David said Bob was speaking about God's love in perfect German. At this point, Richard radioed (walkie-talkie) Larry and asked if Bob knew any foreign languages. So Larry asked, but Bob said he only took Spanish in High School. And he failed it!

Once David heard this, he decided to meet Bob. 'Where'd you learn German?' he asked. Bob laughed and said, 'I don't know German. I did good just passing English in High School!'

David was amazed, since he was involved with a church divided over the issue of tongues. David actually led the faction that believed tongues were not for today. Yet after witnessing Bob's baptism, David asked for prayer to receive the baptism in the Holy Spirit. David and his wife were filled with the Spirit that day and spoke in tongues. A few weeks later, David called Richard and told him that his testimony helped reconcile his church.

Sources:

Larry Boan, Administrative Pastor, Central Assembly of God, Vero Beach, FL.

Dr Charles H. Gaulden, Associate Professor of Religion, Southeastern University, Lakeland, FL. Dr Gaulden worked with Operation Beachhead during this time and witnessed the event.

Richard E. Taylor, Director, Operation Beachhead, Inc., Rock Hill, SC.

Shirley Wallace, 'Operation Beachhead', *The Pentecostal Evangel* 3143 (Aug 18, 1974), pp. 16-17.

Marc Williams, Evergreen, AL. Marc worked with Operation Beachhead during this time and witnessed the event.

GREEK

If I Speak in Tongues ...

Language: Koine Greek
Location: Ryde, Isle of Wight, England
Date: May 1972

One Sunday morning at the Elim Pentecostal Church in Ryde, Margaret Watkins gave a message in tongues. The church's pastor, Dr Ian Hall, immediately recognized the tongue. Under the inspiration of the Spirit, Margaret uttered 1 Corinthians 13 in Koine Greek, the language of the New Testament.

After she finished, one of the church members named Fred Dives opened his Bible, turned to 1 Corinthians and started reading chapter 13. One of the deacons approached Pastor Hall and whispered, 'Pastor, stop him! We need the interpretation before any Scripture reading'. But Pastor Hall told him he would soon explain.

When Fred finished, Pastor Hall explained what happened. He told the congregation while Margaret spoke in tongues, he had his Greek New Testament open to 1 Corinthians 13. As she uttered her message, Pastor Hall followed along word for word. Fred's reading of 1 Corinthians actually provided the interpretation.

The Spirit's presence was truly powerful that morning, but what happened then was only a precursor for the spiritual awakening soon coming to the Isle of Wight. Two and a half months later, revival broke out at the church, eventually sweeping over the entire Island.

Source:

Dr Ian and Sheila Hall, Assemblies of God World Missions (retired). Dr Hall is the Dean, Minnesota District of the Assemblies of God School of Ministry.

Where'd You Learn Greek?

Language: Greek
Location: Small town north of Miami, FL
Date: Summer 1967

Bob Reid was the Athletic Director and head basketball coach at Southern California College (now Vanguard University) in the late-1960s. In the summers, he was also the Director of the Caribbean YWAM (Youth With A Mission). During his tenure, he would take a team of college-age men and women for an evangelistic tour of six Caribbean islands: Antigua, Dominica, St. Lucia, St. Vincent, Grenada, and Trinidad.

On their way to the Caribbean in 1967, Bob drove the YWAM school bus from California straight through to Florida, their final stop before boarding a ship for Antigua. When they arrived, he discovered the need to have some dental work done before leaving for three months. So his hosts dropped him off at the dentist and told him they would pick him up later.

When Bob was finished though, the Lord told him to *walk* back to their house. He thought the Lord had something for him to do, so he started his journey down the sidewalk, praying in the Spirit for an opportunity to witness to someone.

He walked about five blocks but did not see anyone on his side of the street. Then as he continued, he saw an old man outdoors trimming palm trees. He approached the man and began sharing the gospel with him. Yet the man never said a word. He just moved his wheelbarrow from tree to tree.

Finally, the man pushed his wheelbarrow up the walkway to his home and disappeared up the steps. As Bob continued sharing the gospel, the old man stuck his head out of the doorway on the porch. At that moment, Bob suddenly began speaking in tongues. The old man would disappear into the house and then reappear in the doorway. Bob continued speaking in tongues every time he would poke his head out.

After five minutes of this back-and-forth, the old man invited Bob into his home. The old man listened to Bob for 45 minutes and then gave his heart to the Lord.

Before leaving, Bob shook hands with the old man, who thanked him for leading him to Christ. As Bob walked out, the old man asked, 'Where'd you learn Greek?'

'What are you talking about?' Bob asked.

'You know, when you were standing on the steps, you quit talking to me in English and started sharing the gospel in Greek', the old man replied.

But Bob told him he did not know Greek, he was actually speaking in tongues by the power of the Holy Spirit. As Bob walked away, he praised the Lord for the awesome miracle he had witnessed.

Sources:

Dennis G. Lindsay, President, Christ for the Nations Institute, Dallas, TX. President Lindsay did not witness the event first-hand, but was on the summer Caribbean YWAM trip with Coach Reid's team. He remembers hearing the story.

Bob Reid, President, Faith Tech Ministries & International Bible Schools, Lansing, MI.

HEBREW

Baruch HaShem

Language: Hebrew
Location: London, Ontario
Date: Summer 1994

Michael Greenberg and his wife, Linda, attended a baptismal service for a friend's son at London Gospel Temple. While the congregation worshiped, some members began praying in tongues. Michael was Jewish, so this was new to him. 'What are they doing?' he asked his wife.

'They're praying in tongues', Linda replied.

'The woman in front of me is speaking Hebrew', Michael said. 'I recognize some of her words.'

One of the Hebrew phrases was, *'Baruch haShem'*, a popular Hebrew idiom which means, 'Blessed be the Name' (i.e. 'Blessed be the name of the Lord'). After the service, the mother of the baptized boy suggested the Hebrew tongue might have been God's message specifically for him.

The experience really affected Michael. He had yet to accept Jesus as the Messiah, but this experience left a lasting impression with him. During a Passover Seder the following spring, the Lord revealed to him that Jesus was the Lamb of God. Michael then knew that Jesus was the promised Messiah.

Sources:

Michael and Linda Greenberg, London, Ontario.

Robert Smith, Pastor, London Gospel Temple, Ontario.

... the Lord Our God, the Lord Is One

Language: Hebrew
Location: Philadelphia, PA
Date: January 25, 1979

While carpooling to work one year, Wendy Macinskas overheard numerous stories of the miraculous from co-workers. Wendy was skeptical since she was raised Jewish, but eager to see for herself. So she asked a co-worker named Charlene to take her to church.

What she would experience at church would be life changing. In the middle of the service, she heard a man chanting what Jews call the 'Shema': *'Shema Yisrael: Adonai eloheinu, Adonai echad'* ('Hear, O Israel: the Lord our God, the Lord is One'). In Hebrew, he was chanting the Shema to the melody Wendy learned as a child, followed by the rest of the prayer called the 'Ve'ahavta'. 'There's another Jewish person here', Wendy told Charlene.

'No, there isn't', Charlene answered. 'They're all Pennsylvania Dutch. They're all former Mennonites who are baptized in the Holy Spirit'. Yet Wendy insisted she heard someone singing in Hebrew. As they looked around, Wendy pointed to a small, elderly man in a green suit. She told Charlene he was the one singing in Hebrew. 'That's the pastor', Charlene said.

But when they asked if he knew Hebrew, the pastor assured them he had no idea what he was chanting.

Wendy went home that night and prayed, 'God, if you are real, I want to know'.

She heard a voice in her head say, 'Ask me for something'. She knew she was not making it up.

'Okay, I want a baby to put my marriage back together', Wendy replied.

'Ask me "in Jesus' name"', the voice said.

'Oh no, I never did that before', Wendy replied.

'If you don't ask "in Jesus' name"', the voice said, 'you don't get anything'.

Thinking she had nothing to lose, Wendy said to herself, 'Okay, just this once – who will know?' She prayed, 'In Jesus' name ...', and three weeks later she found out she was pregnant with her first child.

Source:

Wendy Macinskas, Philadelphia, PA. Also, see Craig S. Keener, *Miracles: The Credibility of the New Testament Accounts* (vol. 1; Grand Rapids, MI: Baker Academic, 2011), p. 328, n. 126.

Do You Know What He's Singing?

Language: Hebrew
Location: Southern CA
Date: Late-1960s

One night in Southern California, something miraculous happened as Bob Reid, the Athletic Director and Head Basketball Coach at Southern California College (now Vanguard University) and Joe Jordan, an evangelist from Texas, ministered to people in a revival service. During the prayer time, a male vocalist who traveled with them named Randy Posey, suddenly fell to his knees, raised his hands, and began singing aloud in tongues. Bob and Joe had not seen this before, so they just stood there and watched.

Suddenly a man in the audience ran up the aisle to Bob and Joe. 'Do you know what he's singing?' the man asked.

Shaking their heads, they both said 'No'.

'He's singing like a pure Jewish Cantor', the man replied. 'And only five Rabbis in the world could sound that way'.

'How do you know he is singing like a Jewish Cantor?' Joe asked.

'Because I'm a native Jew', the man replied. 'I know the Hebrew language'.

Like those on the Day of Pentecost, the Jewish man was 'cut to the heart'. That day he repented and gave his life to the Lord!

Sources:

Joe Jordan, Evangelist, Joe Jordan Conferences, Shawnee, KS.

Bob Reid, President, Faith Tech Ministries & International Bible Schools, Lansing, MI.

I Didn't Know Your Pastors Spoke Hebrew

Language: Hebrew
Location: St. Louis Park, MN
Date: 1968

G. Raymond Carlson, then president of North Central Bible College (later General Superintendent of the Assemblies of God, 1986–1993), was the guest speaker for the dedication of a new sanctuary at Park Assembly of God. During the ceremony, another guest minister named John Strand gave a message in tongues. Brother Carlson followed with the interpretation, which was an encouraging word from the Lord.

That afternoon, a young Caribbean woman named Kathy Dunn (née Green) attended the service. She worked as a nanny for a Jewish family and decided to invite them to the ceremony. After the service, the Jewish man said innocently, 'I didn't know your pastors spoke Hebrew'. Kathy was amazed. The Jewish man actually understood the tongues spoken by John Strand.

Kathy then explained the baptism in the Holy Spirit and speaking in tongues to him. The Jewish family did not convert, but God had performed a wonderful miracle before their eyes that day.

Sources:

Dorothy Benson, member of Park Assembly of God, St. Louis Park, MN.

Kathy Dunn, Palm Bay, FL.

Dale Embretson, Phoenix, AZ. Dale was present at the service. Also, see Dale Embretson, *We Walk by Faith, Not by Sight* (Plato, MN: Integra, 1991), pp. 53-54.

Edwin Hollen, retired pastor of Park Assembly of God, Minneapolis, MN.

Arvid Kingsriter, Honorary Executive Presbyter and former Assistant Superintendent, Minnesota District of the Assemblies of God. Arvid Kingsriter stood between G. Raymond Carlson and John Strand during the service.

Saved by the Blood of the Lamb

Language: Hebrew
Location: Covington, LA
Date: 1980

One Sunday morning, Marigold Cheshier prepared for worship at Northlake Assembly of God, the church where she and her husband served as pastors. That morning, however, the enemy planted doubts in her head. She started to wonder to herself if she was really saved. Out of obedience though, she went to church ready to praise the Lord.

During the service, the Spirit moved mightily through the congregation as Marigold played the organ. Many came forward to the altar and some were praying in tongues. Before long, Marigold was also praying in tongues.

After the service, a visitor named David Legere asked Marigold if she knew Hebrew. Surprised by this question, Marigold said she had no idea what he was talking about. David then told her she was actually speaking in Hebrew when praying in tongues. Surprised even more by this statement, Marigold inquired as to what was said. David told her she thundered with authority: 'I'm saved by the blood of the Lamb! I'm saved! I belong to him and I'm saved by the blood of the Lamb!'

When Marigold went to church that morning, she started to doubt her own salvation. Yet before she left she had the greatest assurance. As the Apostle Paul testified, 'The Spirit Himself bears witness with our spirit that we are children of God' (Rom. 8.16).

Sources:

Michael and Marigold Cheshier, Assemblies of God Evangelists/Missionaries, Springfield, MO.

David R. Legere, Austin, TX.

… Let Someone Pray in Hebrew

Language: Hebrew
Location: Pasadena, TX
Date: July 1960

Pastor J.R. Goodwin invited an evangelist to preach on the baptism in the Holy Spirit at Pasadena First Assembly of God. Present in the congregation that evening was Rabbi Jack Robbins, who had accepted Jesus as his Messiah six-months earlier. When the evangelist gave the altar call, the Rabbi immediately came forward.

The pastor's wife, however, sensed the Rabbi was skeptical, so she prayed, 'God, you gave the Jews signs. Let someone pray in Hebrew'. Immediately, a man named John Gruver approached the Rabbi, put his hand on his shoulder, and began speaking in tongues.

Yet John was actually speaking in fluent Hebrew. 'I've dreamed a dream that you will go into the big populated places and there you will preach', John said. 'The ones who haven't heard will understand because you, Jacob, son of Rabbi Ezekiel, come in the fullness of the blessing of the gospel of Jesus Christ'.

The utterance shocked the Rabbi. How could John call him by his authentic Hebrew name? And no one in Texas knew his father's name. He turned around and asked John if he knew Hebrew. But John said, 'No'. The Rabbi then told John he was speaking in the highest form of Hebrew, the equivalent to Shakespearian English.

Because of this experience, the Rabbi was completely open to receiving the baptism in the Holy Spirit. That night, the Lord filled him with the Spirit and he spoke in tongues.

Sources:

Joe Jordan, Evangelist, Joe Jordan Conferences, Shawnee, KS. Joe personally witnessed this event. At this time, he was Associate Pastor at First Assembly of God, Pasadena, TX.

John Sherrill, *They Speak with Other Tongues* (Grand Rapids, MI: Chosen Books, 2004), pp. 117-19.

A Baby Named John

Language: Hebrew
Location: Columbus, OH
Date: 1960

One Sunday evening, Pastor Don Neel invited Rabbi Jack Robbins to speak at Fairmore Assembly of God. The Rabbi had converted to Christ and was a Sunday School teacher at the First Methodist Church in Houston, TX. Since he had recently received the baptism in the Holy Spirit, the Full Gospel Business Men's Fellowship asked him to speak at various churches.

The Spirit moved mightily in the service and there was a great time of prayer at the altar. On the ride home that night, Rabbi Robbins told Pastor Neel, 'I understood everything you said while praying in tongues. It was a personal message for you in perfect Hebrew, so I didn't interpret it. You described the birth of your son. He is going to be born tomorrow morning'. Rabbi Robbins then added Pastor Neel's son would be a 'John the Baptist'.

What Rabbi Robbins did not know was that Pastor Neel and his wife, Sophia, had already decided to name their baby, John. When Pastor Neel arrived home, he woke up Sophia and told her what happened. Sophia welcomed the news since she was in her tenth month of pregnancy. The next day, Sophia gave birth to their second son, a beautiful baby boy named John.

Source:

Don and Sophia Neel, retired Assemblies of God pastors, New Iberia, LA.

He Never Studied Hebrew

Language: Hebrew
Location: Chicago, IL
Date: 1964

Pastor Arthur Klaus gave a message in tongues one Sunday evening at Belmost Gospel Church. After a few silent moments, he followed with the interpretation.

After the service, a Jewish woman, who had already accepted Jesus as her Messiah, approached Pastor Klaus. 'Where did you learn Hebrew?' she asked. She thought he must have studied Hebrew since he spoke it fluently and translated perfectly.

Yet Pastor Klaus did not know Hebrew. He could speak English and his native language, German, very well, but he never studied Hebrew.

Source:

Dr Byron Klaus, President, Assemblies of God Theological Seminary, Springfield, MO.

INDONESIAN

Do You Have to See to Believe?

Language: Bahasa Indonesia
Location: South Hills, PA
Date: 1986

Jeannette Persichetti moved to the United States from her native country, Venezuela, in 1985. Before long, she started attending Faith Community Church in Pittsburgh, PA. During the song service one Sunday morning, Jeannette started speaking in tongues. Sitting in front of her was an elderly Asian couple.

As Jeannette spoke in tongues, she heard a question come to mind: 'What if they understand me?' As soon as she heard the question, the couple spun around and asked her if she spoke Bahasa Indonesia (the official language of Indonesia). Startled by the question, Jeannette looked at the couple and simply said, 'No'.

Sixteen years later, Jeannette learned the significance of what happened. A mutual friend had invited both her and her husband and the Asian couple, Daniel and Elizabeth, to dinner one night. They told Jeannette that 16 years prior, their son-in-law was having trouble finding a job. Their daughter had asked for prayer as he waited for a response from a job interview.

Elizabeth struggled with doubt, but God's message to her through Jeannette's tongue was, 'Do you have to see it before you will believe it?' The Lord was teaching her to trust him. As she repented, she knew God was able to provide a job for her son-in-law.

The next day, after hearing this message in the Indonesian language, she received a call from her daughter. Before her daughter could say anything though, she already knew the answer. Her son-in-law got the job and things were going to be fine.

Source:

Bernard and Jeannette Persichetti, Missionaries to Indonesia and Pastors, International English Service South (Indonesia).

ITALIAN

... to Praise the Lord in Italian

Language: Italian
Location: Holland, MI
Date: Mid-1970s

Bob Reid, who had been the Athletic Director and head basket-ball coach for Southern California College (now Vanguard University), returned to his home state, Michigan, in the spring of 1972 to start an evangelistic ministry. Once there, he started holding evangelistic meetings and rallies almost weekly.

During one of his services, a man shared how God called him to missions. After hearing Bob's message though, he realized he had not yet received the baptism in the Holy Spirit. So Bob told him he could receive the baptism in the Holy Spirit right then if his heart was open. He replied affirmatively that he wanted the fullness of the Spirit before making another move.

Bob shared a few biblical passages and then laid hands on him, asking God to fill him with the Spirit. While Bob prayed, the man fell to his knees and began praying aloud. Suddenly, Bob realized the man was speaking Italian. Since Bob grew up with many Italian friends, he easily understood what he heard.

'Does he know Italian?' Bob asked the man's wife.

'No', she replied, 'but he wants to study Italian, since he believes God called him to Italy as a missionary'.

The man's wife then indicated she too desired the baptism in the Holy Spirit, so Bob laid hands on her. The Lord filled her with the Spirit and she started speaking in tongues (though un-recognizable to Bob).

Afterwards the three of them praised God for confirming the man's missionary call to Italy by inspiring him to praise the Lord in Italian!

Source:

Bob Reid, President, Faith Tech Ministries & International Bible Schools, Lansing, MI.

I Was Just the Messenger

Language: Italian
Location: Columbus, OH
Date: 1959

Early one morning, the Holy Spirit woke up Pastor Don Neel and urged him to pray. In prayer, God told Pastor Neel that Hilda Compton, one of his parishioners, was contemplating suicide. He woke his wife, Sophia, and said they had to find Hilda.

Pastor and Sister Neel knocked and knocked on Hilda's front door, but no one answered. As they stood there knocking and waiting, no one came.

'I'm going around to the back door', Pastor Neel said.

Sister Sophia felt a little embarrassed. 'Oh Honey, let's just leave', she said. 'Hilda must not want to be bothered'.

'I know she's here because God told me', Pastor Neel replied. They knocked on the back door, but still no answer.

Still sensing that Hilda did not want to be bothered, Sister Neel said, 'Let's go'.

'No, we're going back to the front door', Pastor Neel replied. And again he started knocking. When Hilda finally came to the door, Pastor Neel said, 'I need to come in. God woke me up and told me that I needed to pray for you'.

Hilda reluctantly invited them in, but said she did not need prayer. Pastor Neel replied, 'God woke me up and told me to come over, so I'm going to pray for you'. He knelt down by her chair and started to seek the Lord. The first two minutes were in English; then he started praying in tongues. When he finished, he noticed Hilda's countenance changed. She looked like a different person.

'Brother Neel, I didn't realize you know my native language, Italian', she exclaimed.

'Hilda, you know I don't speak Italian, but God knew what you needed to hear and I was just the messenger', he replied.

She never revealed what Pastor Neel prayed, but admitted, 'I was thinking about committing suicide'.

Source:

Don and Sophia Neel, retired Assemblies of God pastor, New Iberia, LA.

L'*Amore di Dio!*

Language: Italian
Location: Malaysia
Date: Early-1960s

Loren Cunningham, the founder of YWAM (Youth With A Mission), visited Malaysia as an evangelist in the early-1960s. While working in a mostly ethnically Chinese congregation, someone ran up to him saying, 'Brother Cunningham, come quickly! Someone is speaking in tongues. We think it might be of the devil'.

Loren was a little startled at first, but decided to go check it out. When he got there, he found a teenage girl with her hands raised high and eyes closed. She was speaking Italian, repeating, '*Oh, l'amore di Dio. L'amore di Dio! Il Re è venuta giù!*' ('Oh, the love of God. The love of God! The King is coming down!'). Her utterance was about God's love and the presence of Jesus filling the church that evening.

Loren, who had ministered in Italy, easily recognized the language the young girl spoke. The girl rolled her 'Rs' perfectly just like Italians do. But since the Chinese do not pronounce 'R' in their languages, they thought it was from the devil.

Sources:

Loren Cunningham, Founder, Youth With A Mission, Honolulu, HI.

Janice Cunningham Rogers, Youth With A Mission, Woodcrest Campus, Lindale, TX.

Do You Know Italian?

Language: Italian
Location: Foreston, TX
Date: February 1974

In 1974, Otho Cooley held a revival service in Foreston, TX, a small rural community near Waxahachie. One evening, the Holy Spirit led him to pray for a man named Frank. As Otho prayed, the Spirit moved him to speak in tongues. Frank could not believe what he was hearing. 'Do you speak in Italian?' he asked.

Otho said he did not know Italian, but was only praying in tongues. Frank then told Otho he was actually speaking Italian, his native language, and his message ministered specifically to him.

Source:

Otho Cooley, Assemblies of God World Missions.

But You Just Were …

Language: Italian
Location: Edmonton, Alberta, Canada
Date: 1974

Dan MacTavish led worship at the Peoples Church in Edmonton, Canada in the mid-1970s. During a powerful move of God one evening, many in the congregation began singing in tongues. Dan remained behind the microphone as he joined in with the congregation.

After the service, a young man approached him. 'Where'd you learn Italian?' he asked.

Puzzled, Dan said, 'I don't speak Italian'.

'But you just were', he replied, 'when you were leading worship. You said, *"Portare Gloria a Dio"*' ('Bring glory to God').

Dan was stunned, since he had no idea what language he spoke while singing in tongues.

Source:

Dan MacTavish, Pentecostal Assemblies of Canada missionary, Romania and Eurasia.

In Perfect Italian

Language: Italian
Location: Seven Points, TX
Date: Summer 2000

A mighty outpouring of the Holy Spirit took place at Lakeview Assembly of God one Sunday morning. Members were dancing in the Spirit, some were healed, and many were crying out to the Lord in tongues.

As the Spirit moved, Pastor Don Bell stood and encouraged the church to allow the Spirit to have his way. After his brief admonition, the Spirit began to move again until a hush suddenly fell over the entire congregation. When the congregation fell silent, Reverend Michael Crenshaw, who was a visitor, began singing aloud in tongues for several minutes. Everyone around him was stunned to hear what sounded like a discernable language, though no one had any idea what was sung.

After the service, a missionary approached Reverend Crenshaw and told him he understood much of what he sung in tongues. The missionary explained he originally thought Reverend Crenshaw was speaking in Spanish but then realized he was speaking in perfect Italian.

Sources:

Jeremy Crenshaw, PhD student, Regent University.

Michael Crenshaw, Pastor, First Assembly of God, Eufaula, OK.

JAPANESE

We Interrupt this Program …

Language: Japanese
Location: Radcliff, KY
Date: Mid-1980s

A young Japanese woman was feeling a little down one Sunday morning. 'God, I can't feel you anymore', she prayed. 'If you still love me, when I go to church today tell me in my own language'. After praying, the young woman went off to church, Radcliff First Assembly of God. There God would answer her prayer in miraculous fashion.

In the middle of the service, suddenly everything stopped. A woman named Pauline Holt then burst forth in an utterance of tongues. The interpretation went like this: 'I'm your God. I know where you are and I love you. I'm walking with you. Hold on, victory is yours. I'm still your God'.

After the service, the Japanese woman approached the pastor's wife, Martha Tennison. 'I want to speak to the little black lady who speaks Japanese', she said. 'I heard her speak in Japanese. And then someone repeated in English what she said in Japanese. I heard it twice, once in Japanese and once in English'.

When the two met, the Japanese woman exclaimed, 'You speak Japanese!'

Sister Holt was amazed. 'I can barely speak English, much less Japanese', she replied.

The Japanese woman was confused, so Sister Tennison attempted to explain. 'Have you ever watched TV', she asked, 'and they say "we interrupt this program to bring you a special bulletin?" That is what happened here. The Holy Spirit stopped everything just to bring you a special bulletin'.

The Japanese woman never missed another church service. 'There might be other bulletins for me,' she said, 'and I don't want to miss any'.

Source:

W. Don and Martha Tennison, Assemblies of God Evangelists and former Pastors, Radcliff First Assembly of God, Radcliff, KY.

He Heard the Tongues in Japanese

Language: Japanese
Location: Anchorage, AK
Date: 1974

Before Steve Gray became an Assemblies of God missionary, he served as a soldier in the U.S. Army. While stationed at Fort Richardson, AK, he attended Abbott Loop Christian Center (now Anchorage Christian Center).

On one Sunday morning, a member stood and gave a message in tongues, which was followed by the interpretation. Later that evening, another member stood and gave this testimony, 'This morning, someone gave a message in tongues, which was followed by an interpretation. My Japanese work colleague came to church with me this morning. As he heard the tongues and interpretation, he was astonished because both the person who gave the message and the one who interpreted were not Japanese, since he heard the tongues in perfect Japanese. This afternoon, my friend and I had a long conversation, which concluded with him giving his heart to the Lord'.

This experience had a great impact on Steve, who was newly baptized in the Holy Spirit. When he heard this testimony, he was absolutely convinced of God's miraculous power.

Source:

Steve and Patti Gray, Assemblies of God World Missions.

JAVANESE

Didn't I Give You Another Language?

Language: Javanese
Location: Somewhere between Paramaribo and Moengo,
    Suriname
Date: 1974

Missionary John DeCock picked up a man hitchhiking somewhere between Paramaribo and Moengo, the two largest cities in
Suriname. He tried to strike up a conversation with the man, but
could not get a response. He attempted to speak to him in multiple languages – French, German, Dutch, English, etc. – but the
man just looked at him with a blank face.

Finally, he cried out to the Lord. 'Did I make a mistake by
picking up this hitchhiker?' he asked.

'Didn't I give you another language?' the Lord responded.

'Yes, but …', John thought.

'Well, why don't you use it?' said the Lord.

Thinking there would be no harm, he began speaking in
tongues. To his amazement, the man's expression changed immediately and he started to talk back. From then on, John spoke
in tongues and gave the man time to respond.

They conversed for about 15 minutes. John could not understand a word, but could tell the man was deeply touched.

When the man was ready to get out of the car, he motioned
to be dropped off in Tamanredjo, a Javanese community. Before

getting out, the man started crying. He took both of John's hands in a gesture of thanks.

John never knew what he said, but he had the inner assurance he would see the man again one day in heaven.

Sources:

John and Thelma DeCock, Assemblies of God World Missions (retired). Also, see John DeCock, 'The Old Man Listened When I Spoke in Tongues', *The Pentecostal Evangel* 3177 (Mar 30, 1975), p. 16.

David and Christy Hunt, Assemblies of God World Missions.

KOREAN

She's Praying in Korean!

Language: Korean
Location: Arvin, CA
Date: Mid-1990s

Dr Jim Roane and his wife, Bonnie, witnessed a mighty move of God at a Missionette Camp in Southern California. The Lord's presence was so powerful and real some of the young girls fell 'slain under the power' of the Holy Spirit.

One young girl, a nine-year old named Elizabeth, laid on her back for about half an hour. With her eyes closed, she lifted her arms high in praise and started speaking in tongues. After hearing her, Jim remarked, 'It's a beautiful sight to see such a young girl totally surrendered to the move of God'.

Another young girl named Mari also stood nearby. 'Oh yes, it is', she replied. 'She's praying in Korean!'

Mari easily understood her since she grew up on the Korean mission field.

This surprised Jim. 'What's she saying?' he asked.

'She's praising God', Mira replied.

Elizabeth uttered phrases like, *'Hananimi kamsahamnida'* ('To God be thanks!') and *'Abojisio'* ('Heavenly Father'). When Elizabeth came to herself, Jim asked about her background. She told him she was from California and had never traveled more than a few hundred miles from home.

Sources:

Dr Jim and Bonnie Roane, Assemblies of God World Missions.

John Stetz, Assemblies of God World Missions (retired). Also, see John Stetz, *God's Perfect Timing: A Missionary Family's Adventures in Living by Faith* (Cleveland, TN: Derek, 2008), p. 182.

An Old-Fashioned Prayer Meeting

Language: Korean
Location: Sacramento, CA
Date: August 2010

In the summer of 2010, Dr Del Tarr taught on the Holy Spirit for several weeks at Capital Christian Center. On one occasion, he held an old-fashion prayer meeting for those seeking the baptism in the Holy Spirit.

One of those who came forward was a Korean woman. As she sought the baptism in the Holy Spirit, another woman prayed next to her for encouragement. The Korean woman was surprised to hear her pray in Korean, so she attempted to speak to her. But the woman could not understand a word. As far as the woman knew, she was just speaking in tongues.

Dr Tarr later asked the Korean woman if what happened reminded her of Acts 2, where the onlookers at Pentecost recognized the human languages spoken by the early disciples. She agreed it did. The event had such an impact on her that she yielded to the Lord and immediately received the baptism in the Holy Spirit.

Her American husband – who had been a complete skeptic – then also received the baptism in the Holy Spirit. Having grown up with snake handlers in West Virginia, he believed Pentecostals were irrational and tongues were just gibberish. But once he understood what happened to his wife, he opened his heart and yielded to the Lord.

Source:

Dr Del Tarr, Missions Pastor, Capital Christian Center, Sacramento, CA, and former President and Professor Emeritus, Assemblies of God Theological Seminary, Springfield, MO. Also, see Craig S. Keener, *Miracles: The Credibility of the New*

Testament Accounts (vol. 1; Grand Rapids, MI: Baker Academic, 2011), p. 328, n. 126.

KUSAAL

Jesus' Day Is Coming

Language: Kusaal
Location: Rice Lake, WI
Date: Summer 1965

One Sunday evening at Rice Lake Gospel Tabernacle (now Rice Lake Assembly of God), teenager Andrea Hicks responded to an altar call. Following her prayer, she sat down on the front pew and began praying in tongues for the youth group.

Pastor B.E. Stroud stood nearby and was surprised by what he heard. Andrea spoke in Kusaal, the native language of the Kusasi Tribe of northern Ghana. Pastor Stroud was fluent in Kusaal since he served as a missionary to the Kusasi Tribe in the 1950s. He heard Andrea pray over one of the teenage boys, *'Di ani Yisa kyenna dare, amma o ku toi n kyenna, liki bedigo be ani'* (Jesus' day is coming, and you can't go because it's so dark). She repeated this phrase in an intercessory tone. Then Andrea stood at the altar and exuberantly uttered, *'Di ani Yisa kyenna dare, amaa mam ne dole O'* (Jesus' day is coming, and I'll follow him).

After the service, Pastor Stroud asked Andrea what thoughts were going through her mind while praying. In the first utterance, she prayed for one of the deacon's sons who was not serving the Lord. In the second, the Spirit was dealing with her own commitment to the Lord.

Pastor Stroud then told Andrea she actually spoke in Kusaal when praying in tongues. The news obviously shocked Andrea.

A few weeks later, Andrea joined Pastor Stroud's daughter, Judith, in attending Central Bible College in Springfield, MO.

Sources:

Andrea Fallon, Minneapolis, MN.

Joanne Oftedahl, Assemblies of God World Missions. Joanne witnessed this event as a child.

Bronnie and Annabelle Stroud, retired Assemblies of God pastors, Hilbert, WI.

Judith Stuck, Appleton, WI.

King Jesus' House

Language: Kusaal
Location: Schereville, IN
Date: Late-1970s

Something miraculous took place at a Women's Aglow fellow-ship in Schereville, IN. The guest speaker for the meeting was a Chicago pastor. After a time of worship, the pastor was intro-duced to the fellowship. In a moment of silence, the pastor closed his eyes and uttered a prayer in tongues.

Present in the fellowship that day was Pastor B.E. Stroud and his wife, Annabelle, president of the South Suburban chapter of Women's Aglow. Both Stroud and his wife spent time as mis-sionaries in northern Ghana ministering to the Kusasi Tribe. When the guest speaker prayed in tongues, he spoke in clear Kusaal, the language of the Kasasi Tribe. The Strouds under-stood perfectly what the pastor uttered when he prayed in tongues.

At the conclusion of the service, Pastor Stroud approached the microphone and interpreted what the guest speaker had ear-lier prayed. He told the fellowship that the pastor had spoken in Kusaal, a language that he understood because of his time as a missionary to the Kusasi Tribe. He stated that the guest speaker had uttered, *'Di ani Naba Yisa yiri'*. He told everyone the Kusasi Chief lived in what is called a *'Nayiri'*, which means 'Chief's house'. In English, the appropriate translation for what the pas-tor uttered would be, 'This is Chief Jesus' house' or 'This is King Jesus' house'.

After the explanation, the crowd erupted with praise and ado-ration for what the Lord had done.

Source:

Bronnie and Annabelle Stroud, retired Assemblies of God pastors, Hilbert, WI.

LATIN

The Woman Spoke in Old Latin

Language: Old Latin
Location: Lakeland, FL
Date: January 14, 1996

In 1996, Mark Gardner spoke as a guest missionary for New Life Assembly of God. Since Mark was speaking that day, his Aunt Louise and her fiancé, Ray, visited the service. During the worship, a woman gave a message in tongues. Mark, who is not normally used in interpretation, spoke forth the interpretation.

After the service, Mark had lunch with Louise and Ray. 'Your church was very nice', said Ray. 'What I really like is how you do the eulogies in the Old Latin, and then how you translate it for people who don't understand. In most churches, they don't do that'.

'What in the world are you talking about?' Mark asked.

'The woman spoke in Old Latin and you translated', Ray responded.

'Ray, that's what we call a "message in tongues"', explained Mark. 'It's a gift of the Holy Spirit. And what you heard afterwards is another gift of the Spirit, called "interpretation of tongues"'.

Somewhat baffled, Ray replied, 'Well, I don't know what you call it, but I majored in Latin while studying in the university, and I'm fluent in it. And the woman was speaking in Latin and you translated it very, very well'.

Source:

Mark Gardner, Assemblies of God World Missions.

Sure Enough, Someone Spoke in Tongues

Language: Latin
Location: St. Paul, MN
Date: Early-1980s

One Sunday morning, a young Pentecostal woman decided to take her Catholic boyfriend to Summit Avenue Assembly of God (later Summit Church). Bringing him to church made her a little nervous, knowing the possible exercise of spiritual gifts might scare him away.

Sure enough, Menke Menken, a long-time member, spoke in tongues that morning. The young woman cringed as the message went forward. As she looked at her boyfriend for a response, she saw nothing. Then the interpretation came, and still no response.

After the service, she said, 'Okay, go ahead and tell me what you think'.

'What am I supposed to think?' he asked.

'You know … the message in tongues', she said.

'What message in tongues?' he asked. 'All I heard was a man speaking in Latin and another man translating'.

Shocked by her boyfriend's statement, she decided to explain to him the gifts of tongues and interpretation. She told him neither man knew Latin, but they both spoke by the power of the Holy Spirit.

In the end, what began as a nervous moment for the young woman became a great opportunity for her to explain the power of the baptism in the Holy Spirit and spiritual gifts.

Sources:

Menke Menken, Owatonna, MN.

Charlotte Thompson, St. Paul, MN.

MANDARIN

God Knew Where I Was

Language: Mandarin
Location: Springfield, MO
Date: Fall 1958

Arthur Cao felt a little discouraged and homesick while attending Evangel College (now Evangel University). Yet during a revival service, the Lord spoke specifically to him through a message in tongues and interpretation. When the service concluded, he revealed to some of his classmates what had happened.

'I've been very discouraged', he said. 'I'm away from home and family, in a foreign land, and I just wondered if God knew where I was. The utterance in tongues tonight was in Mandarin, my native language. And the interpretation was a perfect translation. It is such an encouragement and comfort to me – that God knows where I am'.

One of Arthur's classmates was George O. Wood, who would later become the General Superintendent of the Assemblies of God. Dr Wood has stated this experience had a 'remarkable impression' on him as a young college freshman.

Sources:

Robert and Evelyn Bolton, Assemblies of God World Missions (retired). Evelyn was friends with the Cao family.

Dr George O. Wood, General Superintendent, General Council of the Assemblies of God, Springfield, MO. Also, see George

O. Wood, *Living in the Spirit* (Springfield, MO: Gospel Publishing House, 2009), p. 97.

MALAYSIAN

Definitely Malay

Language: Malaysian
Location: Austin, TX
Date: Mid-1990s

During one of the morning services at the Church of Glad Tidings, the Holy Spirit inspired a woman to give a message in tongues. The pastor, then Vic Schober, gave the interpretation as he stood on the platform.

Lydia Gan, an international student at the University of Texas, approached Pastor Vic with a question. 'Did you know the woman who gave the message in tongues spoke in the language of my native country Malaysia?' she asked.

'No, I didn't', he said. 'Tell me about what you heard'.

Lydia, who was working on her PhD in Economics, continued, 'My main language is Chinese, but I understand the Malay language she spoke. She spoke rather quickly, so I wasn't able to make notes on everything. But it was definitely Malay'.

Pastor Vic was very interested in what she shared. 'Since I interpreted what she said, how did I do?' he asked.

'Oh, you did fine', Lydia responded. 'You spoke about love and loving, gifts and giving, and that's what she said'.

Both were excited about the experience. They praised God for the power of the Holy Spirit and were thankful for the woman's message.

Sources:

Vic Schober, former Superintendent, North Texas District of the Assemblies of God.

Lydia Gan, Associate Professor, University of North Carolina, Pembroke, NC.

NORWEGIAN

Obedience to God

Language: Norwegian
Location: New Haven, CT
Date: 1910

While visiting a Danish-Norwegian church, a young woman named Margaret experienced the supernatural power of God. During the service, the Lord gave her a verse of Scripture to quote. When she tried though, the group's leader ignored her and started singing a song.

Feeling a little discouraged, Margaret just returned to her seat. Yet no sooner than she sat down, her hands shot to the heavens and she burst forth in tongues. After the service, a Norwegian woman told her she uttered in Norwegian, 'I speak not to be seen by men, but in obedience to God'.

Source:

Margaret H. Gaines, Church of God World Missions (retired). The Margaret in this story was Margaret Faith Piper Gaines, the mother of Margate H. Gaines. She was a missionary to Japan.

PORTUGUESE

What You Learn in Bible College

Language: Portuguese
Location: Provo, UT
Date: 1987

Students never know what they might learn when they attend Bible College. This was certainly true for some Central Bible College (Assemblies of God) students who traveled to Spanish Fort, Utah for a church-plant. One morning at a prayer meeting in Provo, a young student gave an utterance in tongues. Another student then gave the interpretation, which was praise offered to God.

Both students were surprised to find out Dr Gary Royer, the group's sponsor, had perfectly understood the message in tongues. The message was actually in Portuguese. Dr Royer had been a missionary to Brazil, where Portuguese is the official language. When the student who gave the interpretation heard this, he became a little nervous. He wondered to himself if his interpretation was accurate. But Dr Royer quickly calmed his nerves by stating the interpretation was true to the essence of the message.

That morning, both students learned a valuable lesson. They learned they could trust the Spirit's prompting when moved to use their spiritual gifts.

Source:

Dr Gary Royer, Missions Professor, Southwestern Assemblies of
God University, Waxahachie, TX.

A Need She Had

Language: Portuguese
Location: Fanhoes, Portugal
Date: 1990

In 1990, Byron Klaus preached at the Assemblies of God College in Fanhoes, Portugal. After the service, he prayed for several people, one of whom was a young woman. He prayed intensely in tongues, sensing what he believed was a desperate situation in her life.

Later that evening, a missionary visited Byron in his quarters and told him what the woman reported. She said he had prayed very specifically for an unmentioned need, one she had not shared with anyone. Then she asked, 'When did your American friend learn Portuguese? Why is he using an interpreter?'

Byron was stunned to hear this. He did not know Portuguese or even Spanish at that time. He was simply trusting the Lord and praying in tongues.

Source:

Dr Byron Klaus, President, Assemblies of God Theological Seminary, Springfield, MO.

Millions Will Come to Christ

Language: Portuguese
Location: Buenos Aires, Argentina
Date: July 1982

Something amazing happened when Dr Gary Royer conducted a weekend campaign for a missionary friend in Buenos Aires. It was a Sunday night and the Spirit's presence filled the meeting.

Suddenly a teenage girl stood and began speaking fluent Portuguese. Dr Royer, who was then a missionary to Brazil (where Portuguese is the official language), was stunned. He turned to his friend and asked, 'How does she know Portuguese?'

'She doesn't', claimed his friend. 'She's speaking in tongues'.

Both missionaries sat there spellbound as she prophesied concerning the soon-coming revival that would sweep over Argentina. She said, *'Milhoes virao a Cristo'* ('Millions will come to Christ'). Dr Royer wondered if she really said *'milhoes'* ('millions') or did she say *'milhares'* ('thousands'). But Dr Royer's friend assured him she said *'milhoes'*.

In 1986, the prophesied revival came to Argentina, where millions of Argentinans converted to Christ in the following years.

Source:

Dr Gary Royer, Missions Professor, Southwestern Assemblies of God University, Waxahachie, TX.

QUECHUA

The Living Fountain

Language: Quechua
Location: Durant, FL
Date: Late-1980s

At the old Methodist campgrounds in Durant, FL, evangelist Don Brankel had a marvelous time preaching for members of Pleasant Grove Assembly of God. As the Spirit moved through the service, he began to pray, switching between English and tongues.

Present in the congregation that day was Louis and Libia Grossnickle. Libia spent many years as a missionary in Peru and was shocked by what she heard. When Don prayed in tongues, he was speaking in Quechua, the language of the tribal people in the Andes Mountains. After the service, she told Don, 'I understood every word you just said! You said, "Jesus, you're the living fountain, and I'm drinking from you!"'

Source:

Don Brankel, Assemblies of God Evangelist, Texarkana, AR.

RUSSIAN

Get Right With God

Language: Russian
Location: Pomona, CA
Date: Mid-1930s

A group of would-be thieves decided to rally at a local church before looting the town. When they arrived though, Pastor Huntley was holding a service.

One of the thieves, a Russian, was surprised by something he heard. During the service, Pastor Huntley gave a message in tongues. No interpretation followed, but the Russian understood everything he said.

After the service, the Russian met the pastor at the rear door. 'Do you speak Russian?' he asked.

'No', said Pastor Huntley.

'You spoke beautiful Russian and I understood every word', he said.

The message was specifically for the Russian. 'Get right with God', the utterance declared. 'You're on the road to destruction'.

When Pastor Huntley heard this, he urged the Russian to go to the altar and give his heart to the Lord.

'I can't do that', the Russian said, 'I'm Catholic'.

'That doesn't matter', Pastor Huntley replied,

So both men went to the altar where the Russian was saved and baptized in the Holy Spirit. Following his conversion, the

Russian then brought the other two would-be thieves to church and they were also saved.

Sources:

The Latter Rain 26.11 (August 1935), pp. 22-23.

The Pentecostal Evangel 1115 (September 7, 1935), p. 5.

SPANISH

It's a Miracle

Language: Spanish
Location: near Linares, Mexico
Date: 1980 (approx.)

When Dr Mark Rutland travelled to Mexico on a short-term missions trip, he was in for quite a surprise. With him on the trip were a few American ministers, a translator, the host missionaries, Jim and Helen Mann, and his father-in-law.

The first few days, Dr Rutland preached in some local, rural churches with an interpreter's assistance. The Spirit moved and people were touched by the Lord, but nothing unusual took place. Then one evening, what can only be described as a miracle happened.

The group was scheduled to leave for a small mountain village to preach, but the interpreter did not show up. Though the host missionaries spoke some Spanish, their linguistic ability was not adequate to translate an entire sermon. And Dr Rutland only knew a few Spanish phrases. Yet the group decided to go anyway, hoping someone there could translate for Dr Rutland.

When they arrived, they found a small church of no more than 70 believers. There was no interpreter, so they decided to ask the church's pastor to preach. Before the pastor took the pulpit though, Dr Rutland decided to greet the congregation with his few memorized Spanish phrases. As he spoke, something odd occurred. He realized there was something else he could say in Spanish.

At first, he thought he must have picked it up during previous services. But he just kept speaking. The pastor, who knew Dr Rutland could not speak Spanish, stood and declared to the church that a miracle was happening. As Dr Rutland kept speaking, his father-in-law stood up from the back row and asked, 'What are you doing?'

'It's the Lord!' answered Dr Rutland. 'Something's going on! … It's a miracle, I think'. After that, he just continued to preach his message in Spanish, the whole time understanding what was said. It was as if he now knew Spanish. When he finally gave the altar call, his father-in-law was the first to come forward.

After returning home, Dr Rutland's father-in-law joined a Pentecostal Holiness church in Tallahassee, FL. And though Dr Rutland never took any Spanish courses, the Spanish he spoke that day has never left him.

Source:

Dr Mark Rutland, President, Oral Roberts University, Tulsa, OK.

... in the Language People Understand

Language: Spanish
Location: Costa Rica
Date: June 1996

Kathy Buckles went on a short-term missions trip to Costa Rica with some members of her church, Caring First Assembly of God, Saint Joseph, MO (now Riverside Church). Once she arrived, Kathy prayed, 'Please Lord, let me pray in tongues in the language the people here understand'.

One evening, as she prayed with a distressed woman, Kathy's prayers turned into tongues. She kept praying with the woman until she felt a release from the Lord. When Kathy walked away, the thought came to mind that she had spoken in Spanish when praying for the upset woman.

The next morning, the resident missionary, Rick Ryan, told Kathy that he had been standing nearby as she prayed in tongues the night before. He told her that she had spoken in fluent Spanish, and because of her prayer, the Lord delivered the woman from an evil spirit, saved her, and baptized her in the Holy Spirit.

When Kathy asked the Lord to let her pray in the local language, she had no idea how he would answer her prayer. She simply trusted the Lord and the Holy Spirit did a marvelous miracle.

Sources:

Kathy Buckles, Saint Joseph, MO.

Kent and Leslie Linneweh, Assemblies of God World Missions. Kent was the Youth Pastor at Caring First Assembly of God during this time.

Rick Ryan, Convoy of Hope, Springfield, MO.

I Won't Leave You

Language: Spanish
Location: New Orleans, LA
Date: July 22, 1972

Sister Doris Burns and her husband, Franklin, have served as missionaries to Columbia since 1971. Yet their tenure in Columbia was almost cut short. After just one year on assignment, Sister Burns was stricken gravely ill. The doctors diagnosed her with cancer and she underwent emergency surgery. The Columbian doctors did all they could, but Sister Burns would eventually travel home to the United States for further treatment.

She arrived in New Orleans for more tests in July 1972. Her condition was grave, so the doctors decided to operate immediately. But the surgery proved ineffective.

The doctors then moved Sister Burns to her brother-in-laws' home to recuperate, but she only got worse. On July 22, 1972, Sister Burns was rushed back to the hospital in New Orleans. The doctors wanted to operate but warned the family of the risks. There was a high probability she would not survive.

The entire family gathered around Sister Burns' bedside and started praying. Sister Burns' sister-in-law, Betty Burns, was at the foot of the bed. While the family prayed, she began praying in tongues and then in fluent Spanish: *'Te llamo, te llamo, y no voy a dejarte'* ('I've called you, I've called you, and I won't leave you').

As a missionary to Columbia, Sister Burns obviously knew Spanish and recognized the language. But Betty did not know Spanish. She was simply praying in tongues the whole time. Sister Burns looked up to God and prayed, 'Lord, let me hear that again'.

And again, Betty prayed, *'Te llamo, te llamo, y no voy a dejarte'*. A great peace then settled over Sister Burns.

The doctor then came in to take Sister Burns to surgery. He told her, 'Doris, I'm sorry, but you won't make it'.

But Sister Burns – hanging on to the promise uttered in Betty's tongue – just looked up at him and said, 'Just do your job'.

Hours later the doctor was surprised Sister Burns made it through the operation. 'You're still here', he even said. God's promise held true.

Sister Burns would undergo many other medical trials throughout the next few months, but on December 3, 1972, God spoke to her heart and told her she was totally healed. On Friday, December 10, 1972, the doctors gave her a clean bill of health. Brother and Sister Burns returned to the mission field that January, where they remain presently.

Source:

Franklin and Doris Burns, Burns Ministries International.

Depend on God

Language: Spanish
Location: New Iberia, LA
Date: 1972

Ines Iglesias had just received the baptism in the Holy Spirit when she started to doubt her experience. The enemy told her she was simply making it up when she spoke in tongues. Feeling greatly discouraged, she prayed to God, 'Father, please help me'.

Soon after, Ines went to church, New Iberia First Assembly of God. At the altar, she heard Grandpa Neel, Pastor Don Neel's father, speaking in tongues. With his eyes closed, he prayed in the Spirit as he moved closer to where Ines was praying. Suddenly his tongues turned into Spanish. He said, *'Es necesario. Es necesario. Es necesario aprender a depender de Dios!'* ('It's necessary. It's necessary. It's necessary to learn to depend on God!').

As the only Spanish-speaker present, Ines knew God was speaking directly to her. God had answered her prayer and she never doubted her experience again.

Sources:

Ines Iglesias-Bedolla, Houston, TX.

Paul Neel, Pastor, First Assembly of God, New Iberia, LA.

They Understood His Prayer

Language: Spanish
Location: Chicontepec, Mexico
Date: 1971

Pastor Don Neel went on a short-term missions trip to Mexico with two other men, J.R. Hylton and Sonny Duck. Many thought the trip to be dangerous, so Pastor Neel even made a last will and testament before leaving. The purpose of the trip was to show the 'Jesus Film' to group of Mexican Indians.

When they arrived, an Indian Christian warned them about a Catholic Priest who stirred up the people against 'missionaries'. Sometimes they even stoned people. This was the priest's way of ridding what he called 'little devils'.

In response, Pastor Neel and J.R. prayed against any evil hindrance coming against their ministry. Their prayers proved effective with the priest, but they did run into one snag. When it came time to play the 'Jesus Film', the generator kept breaking down.

So Pastor Neel prayed again, but this time in tongues. To their surprise, the Indian Christians understood his prayer, since his tongue was actually in Spanish.

Once again, his prayers proved effective, since the generator now worked. Pastor Neel showed the 'Jesus Film' and many Mexican Indians came to Christ.

Source:

Don and Sophia Neel, retired Assemblies of God pastors, New Iberia, LA.

... Can I Just Translate It?

Language: Spanish
Location: Brantford, Ontario
Date: January 25, 2010

Something incredible happened when Mark Griffin preached at Freedom House in Brantford, Ontario. After his introduction, the Lord led him to linger in the Spirit's presence for a few moments. As he waited, there was a time of prayer and exhortation. Mark then opened in a prayer of adoration, which eventually turned into intercessory tongues. It is very uncommon for Mark to speak in tongues from the platform, but he sensed a strong need for intercession.

When finished, he opened his eyes to see an excited young man named Keith Cripps standing in front of him. 'I know what you said', Keith exclaimed. 'I know what you said ... can I just translate it?'

Mark glanced towards the pastor, Brian Beattie, who gave him the okay nod. So he handed the microphone to Keith, who told the crowd Mark actually prayed in Spanish. Keith told the crowd he had just returned from an extended missions trip in South America, so he easily recognized Mark's tongue. As it turns out, the message fit perfectly between the worship service and Mark's message. It was a profound confirmation for Mark.

Sources:

Brian Beattie, Pastor, Freedom House, Brantford, Ontario.

Keith Cripps, Brantford, Ontario.

D. Mark Griffin, Pentecostal Assemblies of Canada missionary.

Peculiar Idioms

Language: Spanish
Location: Mitchell, South Dakota
Date: 1945

During the South Dakota District Council of 1945, Pastor Wesley R. Hurst, Jr. uttered a message in tongues. Lloyd Wead, a rural 'cowboy' pastor, then gave the interpretation.

After the service, Henry and Rosalyn Mock, Assemblies of God missionaries to Cuba, rushed over to Pastor Wesley with excitement. They told him his message was in Spanish and Lloyd's interpretation was remarkably accurate. The Mocks were especially amazed since the tongue actually contained peculiar idioms used only in Manacas, Cuba, the place where they served.

Excited by the Mock's testimony, Pastor Wesley, who had been experiencing 'struggles and questions', praised the Lord for the confirmation of the Holy Spirit's miraculous power. As one can imagine, this experience had a long-lasting impact on Pastor Wesley, who would eventually become a foreign missionary to Tanzania (1952-1959), where he established a Bible School and helped form the Tanzanian Assemblies of God. In 1960, he returned stateside to become the secretary of promotions for the Assemblies of God Division of Foreign Missions. Then from 1970 until his heavenly homecoming in 1987, he served as the Missions Field Director for the Far East.

Sources:

Jhan Hurst, Assemblies of God World Missions.

Wesley R. Hurst, Jr., 'A Cherished Spiritual Heritage', *The Pentecostal Evangel* 2605 (April 12, 1964), pp. 14-15, 29 (15, 29).

Gloria, Gloria!

Language: Spanish
Location: Tinton Falls, NJ
Date: 1975

Debbie Martinez was not a Christian very long before she heard someone speaking in tongues for the first time. While in attendance at Glad Tidings Assembly of God, she heard a young woman saying, *'Gloria, Gloria, mi alma te alaba!'* which is Spanish for 'Glory, glory, my soul praises You!' The funny thing is the young woman did not know Spanish. She was just speaking in tongues. Debbie had studied at the University of Puerto Rico years before, so she easily recognized the young woman's utterance.

This experience so moved Debbie she decided to seek the baptism in the Holy Spirit. A few days later, her pastor prayed for her and she received the baptism in the Holy Spirit with the initial evidence of speaking in tongues.

The following year, Debbie attended Southeastern Bible College of the Assemblies of God (now Southeastern University). While there, she attended Tabernaculo de la Fe, a Spanish church in Tampa, FL. One Sunday, she heard the minister cry out, *'Mi alma te alaba! mi alma te alaba!'* ('My soul praises you! My soul praises you!'). Suddenly Debbie remembered the utterance in tongues she heard at Glad Tidings. She now realized why God allowed her to learn Spanish all those years before. Right then and there she decided to dedicate her life as a missionary.

Debbie and her husband, Mitch, currently service as Assemblies of God missionaries to the Dominican Republic.

Source:

Mitch and Debbie Martinez, Assemblies of God World Missions.

TAMIL

Mission: Confirmed

Language: Tamil
Location: Waxahachie, TX
Date: 2005

Every summer, Dr Doyle Jones, the former Missions Director for Southwestern Assemblies of God University (SAGU), would take some of his students on a foreign missions trip. In 1998, a former student of Jones, missionary Chad Germany, asked him to travel to India. But Dr Jones was undecided on whether to go to India or another country.

Then one day something miraculous occurred. Dr Jawahar Samuel from Coimbatur, India, preached in the SAGU chapel. Another professor, Dr Sheba Kulothungan (also from Coimbatur) acted as his interpreter. There was a great move of the Spirit and many came forward for prayer.

During this time, Dr Samuel prayed for Dr Jones. Rather than falling slain in the Spirit – as did most in attendance – Dr Jones began speaking in tongues. Dr Samuel became visibly excited when he heard this. When Dr Jones finished praying, both Dr Samuel and Dr Kulothungan told him he was praising God in their native language. They heard him speak in Tamil without even a hint of an accent. One of the professors, Dr Adonna Otwell, was standing behind Dr Jones when this happened. Knowing he was contemplating going to India, she queried, 'Did you need a confirmation?' and laughed.

Later Dr Jones wrote Chad Germany an e-mail explaining what had happened. Chad replied, 'I just prayed and said, "God, if you want Dr Jones and a team to come to India this summer, speak clearly"'.

Obviously, God spoke clearly. Jones and his team went to India the next summer and started a church in Madurai, India that is still thriving to this day.

Sources:

Chad Germany, Professor and Director of World Missions, Southwestern Assemblies of God University, Waxahachie, TX.

Dr Doyle Jones, International Evangelist and Founder, Doyle Jones Ministries, Waxahachie, TX. Also, see Doyle Jones, *Be Filled with the Spirit: Powerful, Life-Changing Instructions for a Spirit-Filled Life* (Mustang, OK: Tate, 2006), pp. 54-55.

Dr Sheba Kulothungan, Arlington, TX.

Dr Adonna Otwell, Department Chair, General Studies, Southwestern Assemblies of God University, Waxahachie, TX.

URDU

You Want to Know What She Said, Right?

Language: Urdu
Location: Austin, TX
Date: Early-1970s

While attending a Catholic 'Life in the Spirit' meeting, Cotton Rivers witnessed something truly amazing. Two priests were present at this particular event, one was Spirit-filled and the other was not.

During the service, a woman spoke in tongues. The priest who was not Spirit-filled appeared to be quite skeptical and somewhat irritated by this. 'Well', he barked, 'I suppose you want to know what she said, right?' So he proceeded to tell everyone just what the woman had said.

Everybody was surprised! How did the priest know what was said! He then explained that he had been a missionary in Pakistan for five years and he understood the Pakistani language the woman uttered.

When this priest learned the woman did not understand a word of what she uttered, he was truly amazed.

Source:

Cotton and Ann Rivers, Austin, TX. Cotton and Ann later became members of the Church of Glad Tidings (Assemblies of God), Austin, TX.

VIETNAMESE

My Children Listen to Me

Language: Vietnamese
Location: Fresno, CA
Date: 1994

In 1988, Moses Cao returned to his homeland, Vietnam, to plant churches. After escaping the war-torn country by boat in 1975, he did not know if he would return, but the Lord kept the burden of his native people on his heart.

To raise awareness for his ministry, Moses travelled throughout the United States to raise funds for the persecuted church in Vietnam. While traveling, he spoke at Northeast Assembly of God, Fresno, CA.

At the conclusion of the service, something incredible happened. As the congregation prayed for the Cao family, a woman in attendance named Sandra Kirschner burst forth in tongues. Speaking in Vietnamese, she uttered, *'Cac con hay nghe ta'* ('My children, listen to me').

Continuing to speak in the southern Vietnamese dialect, Sandra gave forth a message of encouragement. Her words were reassuring of the promises and faithfulness of God for both the Vietnamese people and the Cao family. The message inspired Moses, who had been contemplating leaving the ministry.

Then suddenly Sandra's tongue switched from the southern Vietnamese dialect to the north's. Crying out for the people of northern Vietnam, she pledged that the gospel would also be proclaimed to them.

Following this miraculous event, Moses returned to Vietnam for a Leadership Conference. During one of the sessions, Moses shared Sandra's message and then called for anyone willing to take the gospel into northern Vietnam.

Several Vietnamese brothers said they were willing to go, including Truong Giang (who would later become the District Superintendent of northern Vietnam). The government eventually caught and imprisoned three of those who left for the north. Many Christian were tortured for their faith during this time, but they all recalled the story Moses told. They remembered God's message of encouragement through Sister Kirschner's tongue.

Since then, thousands of northern Vietnamese have accepted the gospel. On November 19, 2009, the communist government of Vietnam officially recognized the Assemblies of God.

Sources:

S. Michael Bruton, Pastor, Northeast Assembly of God, Fresno, CA.

Moses Cao, Pastor, First Vietnamese Assembly of God, Westminster, CA.

Sandra Kirschner, Fresno, CA.

Thomas E. Trask and Wayne I. Goodall, *The Blessing: Experience the Power of the Holy Spirit Today* (Grand Rapids, MI: Zondervan, 1998), pp. 28-29.

ZULU

Clickety-Clack

Language: Zulu
Location: Minneapolis, MN
Date: Spring 1946

While attending North Central Bible School (now North Central University), Merlin Lund prayed for the baptism in the Holy Spirit. Time after time, he sought the Lord but nothing happened. Then one day in prayer, he started making clicking sounds. The noise surprised everyone, but most told him, 'That's not the Holy Ghost. Just come back tomorrow and we'll continue praying'.

After a year, something then unusual happened. A visiting missionary heard Merlin make the clicking sounds and, as one eyewitness put it, 'about went into orbit'. 'Oh, if you can hear how he's praising the Lord', the missionary exclaimed. The visiting missionary recognized the clicks as Zulu.

Brother Merlin would eventually move to South Africa as a missionary and minister among the different tribes there, including the Zulu.

Sources:

Eldeth Adkins, Columbia Heights, MN. Eldeth and Merlin were classmates at North Central. She was present when the missionary recognized Merlin's tongue.

Edwin Hollen, retired pastor of Park Assembly of God, Minneapolis, MN. Pastor Ed remembers hearing Merlin tell this story when he itinerated.

Sheryl Nesset, Minneapolis, MN. Sheryl is Merlin's daughter and remembers him telling this story.

UNKNOWN AND MIXED

After the Service

Language: Portuguese and Spanish
Location: New Orleans, LA
Date: Early-1970s

During the early 1970s, New Orleans First Assembly of God experienced great revival under the leadership of Pastor Marvin Gorman. After one of the evening services, a woman who had just received the baptism in the Holy Spirit sat in her pew and continued to speak in tongues. Another member, a woman from Cuba who was fluent in at least three languages, sat in a pew behind her.

By this time, one of the associate pastors, Douglas Fulenwider, went into the sanctuary to lock up. Walking by the two women, he noticed the Cuban woman was smiling. He paused for a moment as she told him the woman sitting in front of her was speaking Portuguese, extolling God.

This amazed Pastor Doug, but what happened next was even more amazing. After a few minutes, the Cuban woman told him the woman was now speaking in Spanish with the same type of praise and adoration for the Lord. This went on for several minutes while Pastor Doug prepared to lock-up the church for the night.

Source:

Douglas E. Fulenwider, Superintendent, Louisiana District of the Assemblies of God.

I Understood Everything

Language: Unknown
Location: Waxahachie, TX
Date: 1947

Don Neel had a memorable experience when attending South-western Bible Institute (now Southwestern Assemblies of God University). One day in band class, they had a prayer meeting and Don started praying in tongues. The only other time this happened was when he initially received the baptism in the Holy Spirit at age 13.

Standing near him was his professor of Romance Languages (Spanish, Portuguese, and French), Briggs P. Dingham. Professor Dingham had been a Salvation Army Officer who joined the Assemblies of God after receiving the baptism in the Holy Spirit. When Don finished praying, Professor Dinham told him, 'I've always wanted to hear someone praying in a language I could understand. And I understood everything you said'.

Since Don only spoke in tongues one other time, he had started to doubt his experience. But that day in class, Professor Dingham confirmed his experience with speaking in tongues.

Don would eventually pastor in Brenham, TX, Columbus, OH, Port Isabel, TX, and New Iberia, LA. While pastoring in southern Louisiana, he saw great revival among the youth as many gave their hearts to the Lord and received the baptism in the Holy Spirit.

Source:

Don and Sophia Neel, retired Assemblies of God pastors, New Iberia, LA.

I'm Glad Someone Understands

Language: Unknown Native America
Location: Quakertown, PA
Date: Fall 1978

Doug Olena ministered at Adullam's Cave, a coffee house located in a church basement in southeast Pennsylvania. While others would witness on the streets, he would usually pray through the night.

One evening in prayer, he witnessed some of the other workers surrounding a young man, whom he later found out was Native American, in front of the church. As the man tried to wander away, the group followed him. The young man looked harried. So Doug decided to do something, since he did not want the young man to be offended at the overzealousness of the other workers.

Doug went outside and stood for a moment. The young man then said something in another language. By the inflection in his voice, it appeared to be a question. Immediately Doug felt led by the Spirit to speak in tongues.

What happened next was truly amazing. The man said, 'I'm really glad someone understands me'. Evidently, he recognized what Doug said. After that, he appeared more comfortable and listened to the others for a while.

Before leaving, Doug spoke in tongues again to the man; this time as if to say farewell. The man was not surprised. He just looked back at Doug and simply said, 'Goodbye'.

Source:

Dr Douglas F. Olena, Adjunct Professor of Theology and Philosophy, Evangel University, Springfield, MO.

... He Prayed for China

Language: Spanish and Hindustani
Location: Superior, WI
Date: 1941

In 1941, Bud Abbott led a Wednesday evening prayer meeting at Central Assembly of God. During one of the meetings, a deacon named Louis Ackley started praying quietly in tongues. The group fell silent as they listened to his prayer for about ten minutes.

When he finished, a young man, who had studied Spanish, told the group something truly amazing. 'This man has been praying for China in perfect Spanish', he said. 'He has been praying for the Christians in China, naming provinces. The Christians in each province have been the burden of his prayer'. After hearing this, the group praised the Lord for the presence of the Holy Spirit.

Later that evening, Louis began praying again in tongues. Feeling a sense to intercede, he just yielded to the Holy Spirit's power. When he concluded, a visiting nurse, who had been a missionary to India, asked to speak. 'I'm not a Pentecostal', she said. 'I don't understand your worship, but as this man prayed I understood him, for he prayed in perfect Hindustani, and again he prayed for China. He prayed for the provinces of China and for the Christians in each of these provinces. He indicated in his prayer that great trouble would face these people, and that they would need the comforting power of the Holy Spirit'.

This announcement stunned everyone in attendance. Again, the group praised the Lord for the presence of the Holy Spirit. Although Louis had no idea what language or languages he was speaking while praying, he simply surrendered to the Spirit's prompting. As the Apostle Paul declared, 'Pray in the Spirit on all occasions ... praying for all of the Lord's people' (Eph. 6.18).

Sources:

Bud Abbott, Minneapolis, MN.

Jhan Hurst, Assemblies of God World Missions.

Wesley R. Hurst, Jr., 'A Cherished Spiritual Heritage', *The Pentecostal Evangel* 2605 (April 12, 1964), pp. 14-15, 29 (15).

Charles and Myrna Skaggs, Chino, CA. Myrna is the granddaughter of Louis Ackley.

A Rare Dialect

> Language: Unknown
> Location: Singapore
> Date: Summer 1993

In 1993, Dr Larry Goodrich traveled to Singapore on a summer ministry trip. As he waited to be introduced one Sunday morning, a woman in the far back of the crowded sanctuary began speaking in tongues. After a few moments, Dr Goodrich interpreted the message, which stated God's salvation was available to everyone, regardless of their past.

Following the message, Dr Goodrich prepared to preach his sermon. When he walked toward the pulpit, he noticed four Buddhist Monks in the congregation, dressed in full garb, talking very excitedly to one of the interpreters.

When Dr Goodrich concluded the service, the four monks and the interpreter rushed to the altar. With the interpreter's assistance, the monks questioned Dr Goodrich about the woman who spoke in tongues and his ability to translate. Apparently, the woman spoke in a very rare dialect used only in monasteries. Dr Goodrich told the monks he did not know the language, but God had given him the words to say. The interpreter then told the monks Dr Goodrich's interpretation was remarkably accurate. Truly amazed by this miracle, the four monks repented of their past ways and surrendered their hearts to the Lord.

Source:

Dr Larry Goodrich, Dean, College of Arts and Professions, Southwestern Assemblies of God University, Waxahachie, TX.

I Understand

Language: Unknown
Location: Petra, Jordan
Date: Late-1970s

Over the years, Vic and Naomi Schober participated in a number of tours throughout the nations of Egypt, Jordan, and Israel. On one trip, they experienced something they would never forget.

Traveling on horseback through the very narrow valley leading to and from the hidden city of Petra, Naomi tried conversing with their teenage Jordanian guide. She attempted to speak English at first, but his expression indicated he did not understand. After a couple of minutes, she just decided to sing songs of praise to the Lord.

After several choruses, the Holy Spirit moved Naomi to speak and sing aloud in tongues. When she did, the young man surprised her by responding, apparently in his own native language. She spoke again, and again he answered her.

This dialogue continued for about ten minutes. When they made their way out of the narrow gorge, Naomi dismounted from her horse. As she started to walk away, the Jordanian teenager turned and said in English, 'I understand'.

Naomi Schober did not know what she had said that day, but trusted the Holy Spirit's leading. She simply left the results to God.

Source:

Vic and Naomi Schober, Round Rock, TX. Vic is the former Superintendent, North Texas District of the Assemblies of God.

CONCLUSION

Since the Azusa Street Revival, the topic of speaking in 'other tongues' has attracted much controversy. In the beginning of the revival, skeptics branded tongues as 'weird babel' and 'strange utterances'.[1] More than 100 years have now passed and many still level the same criticism. To most, tongues are nothing more than mere gibberish.

The accounts presented in this book, however, challenge that notion. Testimony after testimony is offered here as evidence of the Holy Spirit inspiring believers to speak or pray in real, authentic languages (and in some rare cases, actually evangelize in real, authentic languages). Whether it is a teenager speaking Apache or a pastor uttering Hebrew, the conclusion is same: *the accounts recorded in this book authenticate the baptism in the Holy Spirit and speaking in 'other tongues'.*

In the end, my hope is that reading these accounts creates a desire for spiritual renewal in the contemporary Pentecostal Church, where currently only 51 percent of American adherents speak in tongues?[2] To the preacher, I say that we must continue to proclaim the doctrine of the baptism in the Holy Spirit (*with* tongues as the initial evidence). To the seeker, I offer a scriptural word of encouragement: 'For everyone who asks receives, and he who seeks finds …' (Lk. 11.9). To the Church, I say that we must not lose the wonder. Miracles are not just a thing of the past. The same God who baptized the disciples in the Spirit on the Day of Pentecost is still doing so today. All over the globe, the Lord fills believers with the Holy Spirit and they speak in

---

[1] *Los Angeles Daily Times* (April 18, 1906), p. 1.

[2] Adrienne S. Gaines, 'Study: Many Pentecostals Don't Speak in Tongues', *Charisma* 11.12 (December 2006), p. 18.

tongues, often as onlookers raise the same question they did on Day of Pentecost: '... how is it that we each hear *them* in our own language to which we were born?' (Acts 2.8 NASB).

Index of Biblical References

Index of Names

Made in the USA
Coppell, TX
24 June 2023

18453418R00085